SATIN PUMPS

THE MOONLIT MURDER THAT MESMERIZED THE NATION

STEVE KOSAREFF

WILDBLUE
PRESS

WildBluePress.com

SATIN PUMPS published by:
WILDBLUE PRESS
P.O. Box 102440
Denver, Colorado 80250

WILDBLUE PRESS is registered at the U.S. Patent and Trademark Offices.

ISBN 978-1-952225-49-9 Trade Paperback
ISBN 978-1-952225-48-2 eBook

Cover design © 2021 WildBlue Press. All rights reserved.

Book Cover Design by Vila Design

Interior Formatting by Elijah Toten
www.totencreative.com

SATIN PUMPS

THE MOONLIT MURDER THAT MESMERIZED THE NATION

For those who I have lost
My mother and father, Susan and John Kosareff

And best friends,
Larry Sleigh
Denis Resseguie
Kyle Counts

And those still around to share a story, a tear or a laugh
My companion, Paul L'Esperance
My sister, Diane Kosareff Maza
And my second mother, Betty Sleigh

In my heart
Forever

Table of Contents

FOREWORD

Like millions of other Americans who have lost their mothers, I'm standing in front of my parents' side-by-side gravesites. Although they passed away five years apart, my parents share a large double in-ground headstone, which I designed, packing as much of our family's life and their photos as I could within its borders. I must have done a pretty decent job because it draws strolling visitors who admire its unique, illustrated storytelling, which stands out from other nearby headstones. My parents rest dead center among the one hundred and twenty acres of Oakdale Memorial Park in Glendora, about forty miles east of Los Angeles. As the headstone attests, their shared gravesite is just two miles west of our former sixty-year family home in nearby Charter Oak.

Oakdale's origins date back to 1890 when the area's first Civil War veterans, who had come to the Golden State to make their fortune, began to die and needed a place to be buried. My parents are in a newer section of the cemetery, surrounded by many Latino gang members who were gunned down in their prime, most of them well under forty. Mom and Dad, resting under their shared pinkish-marble slate, are the unofficial queen and king of these young men. Buried under drab charcoal gray headstones, they were unable to think outside the boxes their lives were to escape only to end up in other boxes in the ground. Between the buried Civil War veterans and the Latino gang members is my childhood, a Southern California midcentury cocktail with a twist of murder.

Many of my family's friends and relatives who once lived in nearby communities are also buried at Oakdale. So is our family doctor, Raymond Bernard Finch. Finch was known by the moniker Bernie, as in "just call me Bernie," which he was often heard to say, warmly introducing himself when meeting someone outside his medical practice. In 1961, Dr. Finch was convicted of murdering his wife Barbara and sentenced to a life term in prison. When he passed away from natural causes in 1995, he was buried—banished actually—across the cemetery road from his grandfather, Thomas E. Finch, a revered founding father of the adjacent city of Covina. Thomas' large standing headstone is a testament to his stature and power as one of the area's prominent businessmen in the 1890s. His grandson Bernie's is a flat, undistinguished, in-ground stone disguised to keep the public from visiting, identified with a first name few knew outside the family.

Bernie's headstone also purposely leaves out his more recognizable middle name, Bernard, which once screamed from newspaper headlines, radios, and television sets sixty years ago. Most people who were alive at the time of Barbara Finch's death and have some recollection of it would be hard pressed to make the connection looking at Bernie's headstone. His family would just as soon you didn't either. The public humiliation and stank of a son, brother, and father who conspired with his paramour medical assistant, Carole Ann Tregoff, and others to murder his wife still swirls like steam above a boiling sulfurous pool over the Eastern San Gabriel Valley sixty years later. The odor may never leave, even after the last of us alive at the time are dead and buried at Oakdale among the Civil War veterans and Latino gang members.

PART I

The author, age 8 in 1959

CHAPTER 1 – SLEEPING BEAUTIES

Sunday, July 19, 1959

Midnight

West Covina, California

Bernie knew the police would soon be at his home as he sprinted, propelled by moonlight and fear, across the South Hills Country Club greens. He entered a grove of orange trees whose branches reached out to stop him, but ended up only whipping and scratching as he continued on, tripping over irrigation furrows. Eventually, one ditch got the better of him and he lost his footing and took an unscheduled break. Now flat on his back, Bernie caught his breath as the sparkling starscape above took it away. On such a warm summer night in the past, he and Barbara once admired the beauty of similar twinkling man-made lights in the San Gabriel Valley below their West Covina hilltop home. Now he was running away from them, possibly, forever.

Six and a half miles away in Charter Oak, I lay awake in my bedroom sweatbox, too afraid to sleep because the window had been left open by my mother for circulation, which was non-existent. We had just come back from seeing Walt Disney's *Sleeping Beauty* at the Covina Theater. The character Maleficent was frightening, too much so for young children to see in a movie.

In my mind, the open window in my bedroom was a beacon signaling her—or for that matter, any bogeyman who happened to be passing by our family home with a yen to pick up a child to-go. The fear of pure evil possessing my sweaty almost-eight-year-old body was stronger than the unbearable daytime heat which had been trapped like a ghost in our suburban attic. I stayed awake in horrified anticipation of screaming in my high-pitched pre-pubescent voice, when the window screen is removed by my abductor and I am yanked from my sauna prison by a supernatural evil queen or a standard-issue bogeyman.

With thoughts of pursuing police encroaching on the starscape, Bernie gathered himself and continued his run through the grove and eventually found a way out. Seeing a somewhat secluded home with a car in the driveway, he approached. Like many people during the 1950s who did not close windows at night, or lock doors to their homes or cars to prevent them from being broken into or stolen, the owner had been accommodating. Bernie gained easy access to the automobile. Having made his career in medicine and not hot-wiring cars, Bernie was in luck: the owner had left the keys in the ignition. As the car moved down the driveway, Bernie ran over a rubber hose which tripped a bell similar to those used in gas stations to alert attendants. But instead of alerting a gun-toting enraged homeowner to run outside and shoot the thief, owner Carl Mossberg just continued to sit in his living room watching television, assuming someone in his family had just returned home from a late night out.

Bernie aimlessly drove under the stress of his flight from justice and ended up in nearby La Puente. Was it a coincidence that his former medical assistant and current inamorata, Carole Tregoff, whom he abandoned at Barbara's death scene, recently lived in the area with her ex-husband? Was he so confused that he thought she might rendezvous with him at her old home? Or did he momentarily forget that he had installed Carole in an apartment in Las Vegas, where they had driven from earlier that evening to talk to Barbara about a divorce?

Where was Carole anyway?!

If the question occurred to Bernie, the thought was interrupted when he spotted another sleeping home with a car in the driveway. He abandoned his current vehicle and, intentionally or not, blocked neighbor William Booth's driveway. The new car was more fitting Bernie's stature: a red and white 1955 Cadillac. Although an older model, it would do. Owner Leon Surruys, like Carl Mossberg previously, also accommodated Bernie by leaving his car unlocked and the keys in the ignition.

Uninjured on the run, Bernie still drove to nearby West Covina Medical Clinic and Hospital, which he co-owned with his brother-in-law Dr. Franklin Gordon. Booth stepped out of his home onto the porch to leave for work and found Bernie's gift, which was about as welcome as a burning bag of dog excrement. Unable to move his car out of the driveway, Booth called police and reported the vehicle's license plate and registration, something he was very familiar with doing—he also happened to be a Los Angeles police officer.

As Bernie pulled Surruys' Cadillac out of the West Covina Hospital parking lot, he was spotted by patrol officers who were looking for him. He jumped on the San Bernardino Freeway and headed west towards Los Angeles with the officers in pursuit.

From sheer exhaustion of a nocturnal vigilance in my bedroom, I passed out. Neither Maleficent nor the local bogeyman appeared to reach through my bedroom window and grab me, but…they had a new plan. A nightmare. Even though Maleficent had supernatural powers, the mortal bogeyman didn't, and since this was the 1950s, she still deferred to the man. *He* was going to star in my nightmare and be joined by a special guest, a buddy of his. The two men were interchangeable in my mind, or they might have been twins, but I was too frightened to envision more detail.

In my nightmare, there was a rapidly moving conveyor belt that spanned the length of my family's kitchen, straight through to the open back door on the service porch. I was running on the belt in the opposite direction in an ever-losing battle to get away from the creepy bogeymen who waited outside on the patio in gleeful anticipation of grabbing me.

Multiple police cars followed Bernie but he managed to elude them by exiting the freeway, crossing under it, and entering again going in the opposite direction. The number of pursuing police vehicles had grown to twenty and they sped past him, came across a similar looking Cadillac and gave chase. Bernie continued east as the police sped west. They ran the pursued car off the freeway and into the median gravel strip, stirring up rock and dust as the vehicles spun sideways and came to abrupt stops. Officers jumped out of their cars, drew their weapons, and slowly approached the car. One yanked the driver's door open.

A very terrified elderly woman meekly looked up at the officer.

The sun had risen and I was woken by the persistent clinking of a spoon in a glass cup coming from the kitchen on the other side of my bedroom door as my father stirred the cream and sugar in his coffee. Bernie, asleep in the nude in Carole's apartment in Las Vegas without her, was woken by two police detectives shaking the bed. They demanded he confirm his identity. Groggily, he did and they told him to get dressed. They wanted to take him in for questioning. I got out of bed and greeted my father in the kitchen.

My nightmare had ended; Bernie's had just begun.

August 20, 1958 – Bernie and Barbara Finch and actor/director Mark Stevens in happier times pose for the Los Angeles Tennis Club's themed costume party, "Gay Paree." Stevens will later testify for the prosecution during Finch's murder trials.

CHAPTER 2 – SUPERMEN SUMMER

Two deaths in Los Angeles during the summer of 1959 turned adults and children alike into ventriloquists, pulling each other's mouth strings and repeating what they heard *ad infinitum*. For kids, it was George Reeves' on June 16; for adults, it was Barbara Finch's a month later on July 18. In a twist of Hollywood fate, both Reeves' mother and one of Barbara's accused murderers would soon share the same famous Hollywood criminal defense attorney, Jerry Giesler.

Reeves starred in the popular *Adventures of Superman* television series that started production in 1951; it finished the first run of syndication for the sixth season the previous year. Its 104 episodes were still airing daily that summer in most cities across the United States. They would continue to do so for decades, getting a new lease when the last fifty-two episodes produced would begin to air in color in 1966. Reeves was popular as Superman, not because of his skill as an actor nor the character's feats of strength, but because his presence jumped off the screen; a compassionate man who loved and cared about people—most importantly, children. Reeves' real acting ability and character strength were put to the test during public appearances in the hot woolen Superman costume at supermarket and shopping mall openings when he was kicked in the shins (or higher) and punched in the stomach by unruly children but didn't respond in kind.

Reeves died by a suspicious gunshot wound to the back of his head. The coroner was quick to rush judgment, calling it a suicide. But the shell casing found behind his head, bruises on his body, additional bullet holes in the bedroom, the gun found feet from his body, and his girlfriends', Leonore Lemmon and Toni Mannix, odd behavior at the time—and years later—gave credence to the distinct possibility he was murdered. Over sixty years later, his death has never been solved to anyone's satisfaction. Within days of Reeves' death, many children had their own collective theory: despondent and crazed over his series cancelation, Reeves took a running leap off the roof of his home to see if he could fly.[1]

Since few children read newspapers nor were fact checkers, this fantastic suicide scenario made sense and was passed from one child to the next as gospel truth. It was still big news at my eighth birthday party two months later on August 14. My guests delighted each other by putting their own spin on the tale as I looked up at the roof of my family home and silently considered the aerodynamics. Superman *would* know he'd need more than the single story of his Brentwood home to get enough lift to fly. And if he didn't, Sky King *would* have told him.

If only he had asked.

Barbara Finch's thirty-sixth birthday would have occurred five days after mine. Her death the month before engendered a similar style of gossip to Reeves'. Only it wasn't about her jumping off the roof of her home in West Covina (although she may well have considered it as an alternative to staying married to Bernie). No, the gossip about Barbara's death was that she refused to give Bernie a divorce and threatened him with a gun, which she conveniently hid in the red 1957 Chrysler 300-C convertible after she drove into the garage. As the story went, after a failed struggle with Bernie over the gun, she dropped it and ran down the driveway to escape. Bernie caught up with her and they struggled once again with the gun, which he had retrieved to keep out of her hands. During the ensuing brawl, the gun discharged into Barbara and she died on scene. At least that's what my mother told me over the decades when the subject came up. And it would occasionally, because Bernard Finch had not only been our family doctor for nine years, he had delivered me and the oldest of my three younger sisters. My family did not subscribe to a newspaper or news magazine during the time Barbara died nor did my mother know other women who were patients of Dr. Finch, so where did she get her information? She wasn't likely to have asked employees at West Covina Medical Clinic about Barbara's death; in fact, at some point around the time it occurred, as we approached the entrance to the medical center, my mother stopped, turned, and looked at me to make a point, and distinctly told me not to mention Dr. Finch's name once we were inside.

We now had his brother-in-law Dr. Franklin Gordon as our family physician. My mother must have gotten what I would find out decades later to be misinformation from a combination of listening to gossipy neighbors and reading salacious magazine articles at her beauty parlor. Consequently, I believed what she told me over the years, like the children at my birthday party about George Reeves.

Until the day I didn't.

The previous September, Barbara had her own Superman, who, like Lois Lane, she decided to call to her rescue: Jimmy Pappa. Jimmy, twenty-five, a body builder, culture model, and construction worker, was Carole Tregoff's husband. Barbara had already called Jimmy a few times and alerted him to Bernie and Carole's affair, but he paid little attention since the two worked together and had good cause to be spotted in each other's company. Under the pretext of needing help to load her son's midget racer into a borrowed station wagon, Barbara called Jimmy again. Who better than the Superman she knew to help than Jimmy? But Jimmy proved to be more like his Olsen namesake than Superman. As Barbara began to grab the heavy end of the racer with the motor, gallant Jimmy assisted by picking up the lighter one[2]. As they lifted the racer into the car, it was an opportune time for Barbara to ask Jimmy if he knew Bernie and Carole had been spotted together in Palm Springs. Jimmy admitted he had heard that the two had been seen there but believed it was just gossip; besides, they worked together and could have had a legitimate, professional reason for being in the desert town. Maybe Dr. Finch had a patient in Palm Springs who was in need of their help.

Sure…

Barbara was not persuaded by Jimmy's explanation and asked what the two of them were going to do about their spouses' philandering. Jimmy threw Barbara a curveball and asked that if she had proof of her husband's adultery, why didn't she just file for divorce, to which she responded, "Why should I get a divorce? I have it made being married to Dr. Finch." She told him that she had already been through one divorce and didn't want another. As an afterthought Barbara told Jimmy that Carole wasn't even Bernie's first affair.

She failed to tell Jimmy how she knew this.

---

2. Unembarrassed, even years later at the memory, Jimmy would tell the court at the second murder trial that he was amazed by Barbara's strength.

CHAPTER 3 – AMERICA'S CROSSROADS

I was delivered by Dr. Finch as a caesarean birth on August 14, 1951, at 10:01 a.m. at Monrovia Hospital in Monrovia, California. My parents were also born in California, as were my maternal grandparents, but my paternal grandparents came from the Russian Republic of Georgia. All four grandparents were Russian Molokans, but my maternal grandparents rebelled as American teenagers, as they have a habit of doing, and stopped attending church and practicing their parents' faith. Molokans were/are similar to American Pentecostals bound together by dark, brooding fundamental Christian beliefs and a willingness to put their collective nose in someone else's business to make sure they toe the party line. Unlike Pentecostals, however, Molokans share dietary laws with Jews and Muslims. You won't see conservative old-school Molokans eating a honey-baked ham on Easter nor shellfish at a clambake during the Fourth of July.

For most of my life, I thought my family originated in Georgia until a DNA test showed that 95% of my ancestry traces back to Moscow and St. Petersburg. My companion Paul said that maybe I was related to Anastasia and the royal family; but then why did my forbearers end up as poor peasant farmers in Georgia without an interesting story to tell about the search for their heirloom Fabergé eggs?

My paternal grandfather, Michael, was born October 26, 1886, and immigrated to the United States in 1905 as a young man with thousands of other Molokans to escape the Czarist conscription during the war with Japan. Initially, like many Molokans, he landed in the Boyle Heights section of East Los Angeles, noted by Carey McWilliams in his celebrated 1946 book, *Southern California: An Island on the Land.* Boyle Heights was where poor Russians, Jews, and Mexicans lived, and even today the makeup is similar, but with a Latinx majority. I do not know anything about my maternal grandmother Faye Nickolavna because she died in childbirth, as did her baby boy, when my father, John, was just two years old. At the time he was the second youngest of seven children living on a small farm in California's Central Valley near Helm.

My maternal grandmother, Esther Mohoff, was born on August 20, 1913[3], in Los Angeles. Esther lived for a very short time in Guadalupe, Mexico, with her family. There were a series of border crossings she made in early 1927 at thirteen, documented just weeks before and after her wedding to my grandfather, Morris, on March 5 of that year. Esther's family lived on a Molokan communal farm and ranch of approximately a thousand acres not too far from Ensenada. Each of the one hundred families had private plots of land to build homes, as told by her nephew, George Mohoff, in a series of self-published books. While the books celebrated the hard life in Mexico, apparently it was too much for the free-spirited Esther, who decided to get the hell out of Dodge (or Ensenada, in this case), as quickly as possible. She married my grandfather across the Mexican border in Santa Ana, California. Esther's young age and trips back and forth across the border beg the question of whether or not she was with child and had to get married. The marriage license states both were nineteen, providing an exact birthdate for my grandfather but not even a phony one for my grandmother, possibly to cover for an underage girl. Was it a shotgun wedding? I've found no proof of a pregnancy before my mother Susan was born on December 27, 1928. Could there have been a previous pregnancy that ended in miscarriage or stillbirth? I don't know, but why are there so many different birth years listed on documents for my grandmother? It's like someone couldn't keep track of their story to falsify her age.

My maternal grandfather, Morris Alder, was born in Los Angeles in January 1908. I have very fond memories of him, including his penchant for practical jokes (if you're old enough you may remember the plastic poop piles one could buy at local five-and-dime stores). Once, Morris planted one on his living room carpet, pranking and nearly convincing my mother that one of us kids hadn't been able to make it to the bathroom. My grandfather (and grandmother) had a hearty, rollicking laugh, which my mother inherited and I could hear amplified whenever she found something outrageously funny on television. I can still feel its warmth passing through the forced-air heating duct above the living room wall into my bedroom on the other side. I now realize I share their laugh and a pang of loss rises from my gut because it reminds me that the laugh, and possibly even my sense of humor, came from those I love and have lost.

Dr. Finch's paternal widowed great-grandmother, America Catherine (Bradford) Finch, was appropriately named. In 1881, after her husband John William Finch died, she traveled the breadth of the United States, from Virginia to Northern California, to be with her son, Thomas. Thomas had moved to California in 1876 and owned a farm in Dent, an area in Alameda County. America also brought the seven youngest of her eleven children with her. Train travel was possible then but somewhat expensive, even in third-class for a family of eight, and not very comfortable. Although wagon trains were all but gone by time the First Transcontinental Railroad opened in 1876, part or all of the trip could have still been made by covered wagon or stage, making the journey even more difficult for a single parent with a large brood.

In 1862, America's husband William had been drafted into the Confederate Army in Virginia. His draft card states he had blond hair and blue eyes, a trait that would continue in following generations of Finch men, including his son Thomas Enoch, grandson Raymond Ralph, and great-grandson Raymond Bernard. A man of strong convictions against the South's positions, William deserted and joined the Union Army.

Two years after the war ended, America still did not know his whereabouts or even if her husband was still alive. But she soon found out when he surreptitiously returned to avoid being branded and punished as a traitor and to gather the family and quickly move to Grainger, Tennessee. William would pass away in 1880 and America would leave for California the following year.

America moved to Covina in Southern California in 1885 when Thomas bought a forty-acre plum and apricot orchard at the corner of Citrus Avenue and Puente Street, where the first Covina High School would be built in 1897. Historian Donald H. Pflueger wrote in his 1964 book about the city that Thomas was locally noted for having grown a one hundred-pound pumpkin in 1886, as well as drilling the first water well in the area. Thomas also owned large acreage of wheat in an area further south, then known as Rowland. Covina locals took notice and Thomas became one of Covina's founding fathers, managing various aspects of the town's business. He moved into the town proper in 1898 after selling his orchard. It's likely he continued to maintain a second home on his Rowland acreage because voting registration and census records list him and members of his family living there. He swapped and sold properties and businesses so quickly it's hard to keep track of his investments, but in 1900, he partnered with Lambert Ratekin in the Covina Orange Growers Association processing plant for five years. They then purchased a grain milling and farming/ranching supply company on Citrus Avenue in downtown Covina and renamed it the San Gabriel Valley Milling Company. Available historical texts and documents contradict one another, so it's not clear when Thomas owned or co-owned with a son (or sons) or invested in the grocery/ department store across the street called Thomas Finch & Sons. In any event, with his considerable business and land holdings, Thomas Enoch Finch *was* Mr. Covina.

Like his father before him, Thomas took great civic pride in contributing to society. He was a Covina city trustee and responsible at one time for its fire department. Like her son, America was a very active member of the local Church of the Brethren. Her husband William's actions during the Civil War appear to support a membership because he practiced the church's anti-war and anti-slavery tenets. The Brethren share non-violent beliefs similar to Quakers. Subsequent generations of Finches would be members of the Brethren, including America's great-grandson Raymond Bernard who, long after her death, would engage members at gatherings with medical talks when he became a doctor. Decades later, during his confinement in jail, Bernie, awaiting the outcome of the third murder trial, would turn to the Bible and religious books for comfort and protection.

Thomas' son Raymond Ralph Finch (b. 1890) joined his brother Thomas (named for their father) in 1912 in his jewelry store business across the street from their father's grocery/department store. Finch Jewelers was known by the time the brothers sold it in 1952 for its forty-two years of service and its 1916 clock tower, which stood just outside (and where it still stands today) as not only the business's anchor, but the city's. Citizens without timepieces looked to the clock tower to be reassured about the time or to meet someone underneath. Although he co-owned the jewelry store with his brother, Raymond also had a business next door as the city's optometrist.

By the time America died at the age of eighty-seven in 1914, the Finches were not only established in Covina, but elsewhere in Southern California. Three generations were well known and loved by locals for their religious faith, civic responsibility, and success as local entrepreneurs. Nothing less would be expected of succeeding generations, including four years later in 1918 when Raymond Ralph's son, Raymond Bernard (known both as Bernard and Bernie) was born. But something would soon change in the family dynamic for Bernie, and serving the community, having a lot of money, and familial recognition would not be enough for the Prince of Covina.

He wanted to be King of the San Gabriel Valley.

CHAPTER 4 – THE MURDER KIT

When Bernie married Barbara Jean (Reynolds) Daugherty in Las Vegas on Christmas Eve 1951, they had no home to return to from their honeymoon, just their individual apartments. But Bernie had ambitious plans for a new home he was building on what would turn out to be several combined hilltop lots in West Covina. He also designed the house and it would bear, as others would later note, a striking resemblance in its layout to the new West Covina Medical Clinic. The home, like the clinic, was laid out in a U-bolt shape, with three wings. Whereas the clinic centered on a small garden with an exit door off the entrance to administration and business offices, the home was centered on a patio surrounding a rectangular swimming pool. One person noted that the home had a cold, institutional feel to it, like the medical clinic it was modeled on, and even the swimming pool in the center never warmed. It took a year to finish and Bernie, Barbara, and her young daughter (by former husband Lyle Daugherty) Patti Dee moved to their new home in July 1952. Soon thereafter she found out she was pregnant and gave birth to a son, Raymond Bernard Finch Jr. (known in his youth as Raymie and later as an adult, Ray) the following April.

When Bernie's father Raymond retired and he and Thomas sold the jewelry store in 1952, Raymond had already purchased the lot across and just steps down from Bernie's private driveway and built a home for him and his wife, Marian Eva. They wished to enjoy their golden years being close to their son, daughter-in-law, and grandchildren. It was idyllic for a while—that was until Bernie and Barbara began to fight. Raymond could hear them across the driveway, above, inside their home, particularly if he was outside in his backyard.

Why couldn't they work things out?

After all, this was a second marriage for both of them; Bernie and Barbara knew what being married entailed before they decided to tie the knot. Raymond would try to shield Marian from his son and daughter-in-law's sparring by going inside and closing the windows and distracting her. Marian didn't need to worry about Bernie, Barbara, and the kids. She had her own problems: health issues confined her to a wheelchair.

And so it would go for the next several years until that July evening, late at night, that Raymond heard what he later told police was a car backfiring—*twice*—but in his heart, he knew otherwise. He did not want to get out of bed, open the door, and walk outside into a reality there was no turning back from. Maybe in the morning he would wake up and the noise he heard would turn out to be *two* cars backfiring.

However, that following morning, Raymond, an early riser, got out of bed and looked out the living room window over his front yard. There was a police presence in the distance. At least something didn't happen here on his property, he probably thought, but what about Bernie's?

.

CHAPTER 5 – VIVA LAS VEGAS, PART I

The closest I ever got to Las Vegas before I was an adult was the summer of 1970 as a nineteen year old, between my freshman and sophomore years of college. I worked for my father in Death Valley, operating a Caterpillar DH-9 bulldozer, excavating talc from a hilltop mine. The DH-9 was Caterpillar's second largest bulldozer. It was so mammoth that to start the diesel engine, you first had to start a gasoline pony motor to turn it over. My dad, who operated a second bulldozer, and I worked in tandem on a hill that was part of the open pit mine. If either one of us made a wrong move, say spinning a dozer around too quickly on its tracks on just the wrong rock, the machine would lose its footing on the slope and roll over. There were no seatbelts then; there weren't even roll cages.

This would prove fatal within a few years when one of my father's bulldozer operators tried to come off the hill too quickly by cutting corners and flipped over. A 1975 law subsequently required that all new 1976 tractors be equipped with rollover protection structures. My father told me not to tell my mother about the danger. I didn't because I knew the money he was paying me, near what he would pay a professional operator, would pay for my upcoming New York visit to my best friend from college, Denis Resseguie, whose family lived in Lockport, near Buffalo.

Still, I hated the job.

I hated the triple digit heat that made me so sick to my stomach that I had to take a break and seek refuge nearby in the old talc mine shaft; I shared the space with rattlesnakes, where it was only eighty degrees and felt like refrigeration. The snakes stayed in their corner and I in mine.

I hated the desert, having already lived my whole life in the semi-arid, rocky, sandy land of Covina that made me suffer whenever the Santa Ana winds blew dirt and dust up my nose and exploded into allergies in my sinuses.

I hated the desert desolation.

I hated living in a small house trailer without electricity and using a dry ice box that froze tomatoes.

I hated hearing the coyotes howl at night and I hated hearing whatever was scratching between the walls of our trailer, waiting to jump out at me while I slept.

I hated the day's heat trapped in the trailer, which finally cooled to eighty degrees between four and six in the morning, when I finally could sleep without the childhood nightmares of summers past.

I hated the always-hot, makeshift shower outside.

I hated it all so much that when my father, who was no music aficionado, offered that instead of making our weekly Friday evening drive home to Covina one particular weekend, we could drive ninety miles and stay the weekend in Las Vegas to see Elvis Presley at the International Hotel—I turned him down. I was homesick for Covina.

What was I thinking?! Elvis Presley! The King!

Covina?!

Of course, had we gone to see Elvis, and even dressed in our cleanest work clothes, we still would have looked like two old tanned, bearded prospectors, but as long as they let us valet park our mules outside and use talc dust for gambling currency, we would have had a grand old time. I wonder if Dr. Finch ever recommended to my mother that she use talcum powder on my chapped baby bottom.

I'm sure talcum powder was the furthest thing from Bernie's mind eleven summers earlier and ninety miles away sitting in an interrogation room. The Las Vegas sheriffs were in no hurry to question him. They were waiting for his girlfriend, the attractive twenty-two year old Carole Tregoff, to arrive and wanted to interview them concurrently, in separate rooms, in an attempt to prevent the two from collaborating on an alibi.

Earlier, sheriffs had been tipped off that Carole worked as a cocktail waitress in the Copa Lounge at the Sands Hotel by another sheriff in the department. When Detective Hiram Powell found her there, she willingly gave her home address and told him Finch was at her apartment, sleeping. After her shift ended and she returned home, she called the department to inquire about Bernie. Detective Powell asked if he could speak to her and she agreed. He drove over with Lieutenant Detective Ray Gubser and upon entering the apartment, asked if he and his partner could search the home, to which she also agreed. Carole told them she and Finch drove to West Covina the previous night to speak to his wife about a divorce. This nugget piqued the detectives' interests and they asked if they could speak to her downtown. She agreed and the three of them, with a box of Finch's belongings, headed for department headquarters.

After Finch was rousted from bed and taken to the sheriff's department, he told officers that he was in Las Vegas at the time of his wife's death. In another interrogation room, Carole told police that Bernie flew up the previous Friday to see her, contradicting him. She told sheriffs she and Bernie decided to speak with Barbara and convince her to go through with the divorce proceedings, which had been tabled pending a conciliation hearing, scheduled to take place in a few days. Carole and Bernie drove her 1955 white and bronze DeSoto convertible to West Covina and parked it in the South Hills Country Club parking lot down the hill from the Finch home. Once they walked up the hill to the

Finch home, they noticed that Barbara's car was not in the garage, so they waited for her on the front lawn. After she drove into the garage and as Barbara was getting out of the car, she spotted them approaching. She screamed and pulled a gun out of her purse. Carole, scared, ran out of the garage and hid in a bougainvillea bush, where she remained for hours. Carole did not see nor hear what happened after that. Early that morning, she returned to her car and drove back to Las Vegas. Bernie beat her to the apartment by several hours and she found him asleep at 9 a.m. She got ready for work and left.

West Covina detectives escorted Finch back to a Covina jail cell that afternoon. The West Covina Police Department did not have holding facilities at the time, so Finch spent time behind bars in Covina while awaiting his upcoming hearing at Citrus Court. Carole assured police that upon her return to West Covina she would make a statement and appear as a witness at Finch's hearing.

That day, police had already started an intensive search of the grounds surrounding both Finch homes, looking for the gun responsible for Barbara's death. Raymond told reporters gathered on the properties that he heard what he thought was a car backfiring but later realized were two gunshots when he saw police in the area that morning. He added that Bernard had been going to a psychiatrist twice a week for the past three months and had been "off the beam for three or four months and should have been put away." Dr. Franklin Gordon told him that Finch had been "'pulling strange deals around the office.' Dr. Gordon told me that if Bernard kept up with his strange actions that he would have him committed himself."

Dr. Alan Cheesebro, Finch's tennis doubles partner and assistant pastor, summed up Finch succinctly a few days later at, of all places, Barbara's funeral service. "The doctor was very aggressive, strong-minded, and intense in everything

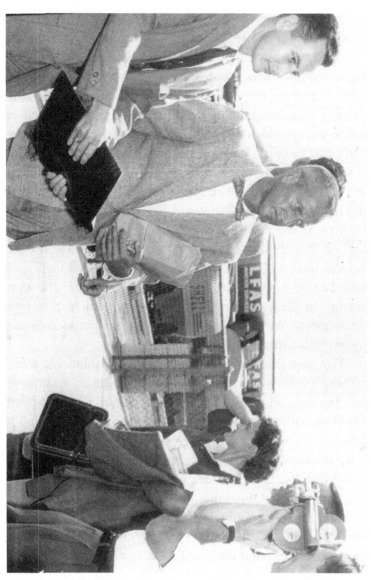

July 20, 1959 – Dr. Bernard Finch arrives back in Los Angeles at Ontario Airport from Las Vegas escorted by West Covina Police Captain William Ryan and Chief Allen Sill (hidden behind Finch).

he did. He had a wonderful nature that would erupt now and then in jagged bluntness, warm reproach, or hot hatred."

The "strange deals/actions" Dr. Gordon referred to were likely Bernie's dalliances with the female staff at the medical center. Instead of having Finch "committed," Gordon and the rest of the medical center board likely relieved him of some of his duties at the medical center the previous year (about a month prior to the new hospital opening) by steering his patients and their families to other doctors, including Gordon himself. Patients likely found out via a form letter stating Dr. Finch was downsizing his practice for other pursuits; it's unlikely those "pursuits" were named, but if Bernie stayed true to form, they were going to be women.

The board's letter also may or may not have mentioned that Finch's partnership in the hospital and clinic would remain but avoided stating this to guarantee the previous loans to build the hospital and maintain a line of credit. This would explain how nine months *before* Barbara died, my second sister Debbie became the first baby born in West Covina Hospital the day after it opened on October 21, 1958, but was *not* delivered by Dr. Finch. She was delivered by Dr. Gordon, who had become our new family doctor.

How much of this Gordon told his wife/Finch's sister, Marian Louise, would have been a fine line to walk. Marian Louise and her younger sister Jane were Bernie's biggest supporters from childhood, next to their father and mother. They had been raised from the beginning knowing Bernie was the chosen one in their family and would soon be beyond the four walls of their home. When Bernie graduated from medical school and began to practice at the Magan Clinic, everyone in the San Gabriel Valley knew it and acted accordingly—from police who stopped him when he was drunkenly speeding and gave him a pass—to the female employees at the medical clinic who jostled with each other to be his next conquest.

How would Marian react if she knew Franklin had torpedoed Bernie to save his own neck—and, by proxy, hers?

Back on the Finches' adjoining properties, Raymond, pent up with emotion covering for Bernie's behavior for years, had been informed by police that the worst was true: Barbara was dead. He was righteously aroused to defend his beautiful, popular, dead daughter-in-law against his errant son. He had plenty to say to reporters and opened with a bombshell: Raymond told them that Bernie and Barbara had fought before but nothing ever happened to the degree like him *shooting her in the back*.

"She fell just a few feet from the front door. Ten more feet and she would have reached the safety of my house. My God, what a tragedy." Raymond's claim that his son shot Barbara in the back couldn't be more damning—until a few days later

Earlier that morning, Raymond, unnoticed by police, walked up to Bernie's front lawn. There he discovered a locked brown leather attaché case and grey alpine hat and picked them up. He continued on to his son's front door. Finding the home unlocked, he entered and, possibly assuming the home had been robbed, headed to a hidden area where family valuables were kept. He opened a silverware case and inside were Barbara's wedding rings. He removed and pocketed them, picked up the silverware case, attaché case, and alpine hat, and exited the home. He walked back to his home on the other side, never stopped nor questioned by police. Five days later, on July 24, he finally gave West Covina Police Detectives Ryan and Hopkinson the alpine hat and the locked leather attaché. As Raymond handed them off, he referred to the attaché as his son's "tennis case" in an effort to convince himself that his son's tennis balls were inside, and, if not, psychically will them into existence.

Why did Raymond keep the attaché so long before turning it over? Did his gut feeling tell him the case contained more nefarious items than tennis balls? Was he considering not giving it to police in an effort to protect his son? If so, what caused him to change his mind?

Raymond was asked where he found the case and hat. The detectives were privately embarrassed that officers, who had been on scene continuously since Barbara's death (including Officer Frank Meehan), hadn't found them lying out in the open.

Although the case was locked, Ryan and Hopkinson were given a set of keys by Las Vegas sheriffs that were found in Finch's wallet. Testing the keys, they found that one opened the case. Ryan and Hopkinson were surprised at what they found inside. They told no one except the district attorney's office, which decided to save the bombshell for Finch's upcoming court hearing. After the big reveal took place, West Covina Police downplayed how the department came to be in possession of the attaché, hoping to deflect attention from their initial mishandling of the case. At the murder trials, Officer Meehan would claim that he either found the case or that Raymond immediately pointed it out to him upon his discovery, as though Raymond had never held it for a few days before giving it up.

Unaware that Raymond had just opened the door to the gas chamber for him by his uncensored statement to reporters, Dr. Bernard Finch slept his first night in a Covina jail cell like a freshly-talcumed baby awaiting his hearing in Citrus Court. He would continue to do so even a few days later, not knowing his father had delivered the attaché case to police.

Eleven summers later in Death Valley, the talc dust had finally settled on my night. My father and I had retired for the evening after having dinner together in the trailer. He was sleeping and I was reading the recently published *The*

Godfather by kerosene lamp. The desert silence was broken once again by something scratching and trying to claw its way out of the trailer wall.

What the hell was that?!

Sonny Corleone had a hair-trigger temper.

And so did Dr. Bernard Finch.

CHAPTER 6 – QUICK DECLINE

The only quick decline Bernie possibly contemplated as he fled through the orange grove the night Barbara died was about how he'd fare in prison. Not so for orange growers, who had been fighting the so-called citrus disease since it had first been discovered in Southern California in 1939. Once-healthy trees would wither and die within two weeks. The disease would even jump trees, indiscriminately killing some in its path while leaving others unscathed. During the forties and early fifties, Quick Decline continued ravaging groves at an alarming rate and no knew how to stop it. Everything science, quackery, and magic could throw at it was tried, but nothing worked. It wasn't until 1946 that scientists finally discovered that the disease was caused by a virus. Then, in 1951, Dr. Robert C. Dickson discovered that the virus was spread by the melon aphid. Although it was known that humans practicing horticulture on the trees spread the virus, none was more insidious than by the aphid. By the time the aphid was discovered, it was too late for the trees fifty years old or more, which were already past their fruit-bearing years. Quick Decline (coupled with skyrocketing property taxes and suburban developers dangling handfuls of cash in their faces) forced growers to play the one good hand they had and sell.

This was how my parents' new model three-bedroom home, The Langham, part of a tract of thirty-eight similar homes developed by brothers Loyd and Albert Meissenburg on ten acres known as Charter Oak Manor #3, "a Subdivision of a portion of the Southeast Quarter of the Northwest

Quarter of Section 8 Township/South Range 9 west of the Subdivision of the Rancho Addition to San Jose and a portion of the Rancho San Jose," came to be in 1956.

I can't find photos of the land when the orange grove existed, when the trees were removed, or as the houses rose from the ashes of the grove. Assuming the two groves across the main thoroughfare from our house, Cienega Avenue, were planted at the same approximate time as the grove my parents' and neighbors' homes replaced, it was likely planted somewhere between 1890 and 1910.

As a child I couldn't have cared less about the history of the two orange groves across Cienega from our home. They were on private property and I do not remember playing among the trees nor stealing oranges. It wasn't until writing this book that I began to investigate the history of citrus production in Southern California, particularly the Covina/Charter Oak area.

The groves across Cienega were distinguishable from each other only by their windbreakers, which were planted to protect them from the vicious cold winds of winter and the dry, hot ones of summer, something their citrus forbearers never suffered in their natural habitat in tropical Southeast Asia.

The grove on the left had tall eucalyptus trees, and the one on the right, towering date palms. Viewing my family's home movies, shot in our patio breezeway with the camera pointed toward Cienega with the orange groves in the background, one sees healthy groves that existed until 1959. In subsequent films, the trees are dead but still standing. Was their death due to Quick Decline or grove owners who gave in to prevailing forces and withheld care? Can't say, but by 1963, the dead trees had been uprooted and replaced by ugly tract homes. In just four short years, the beautiful sylvan view that I didn't appreciate as a child was barely a memory for adults the year President Kennedy was assassinated.

The local groves in Charter Oak, while they existed, were a mysterious place for children to trespass, play, and stick their bare feet in irrigation water as it whooshed through furrows and, hopefully, not trip over them like Bernie Finch. There were also tons of tantalizing ripe oranges before groups of hired Mexican pickers got to them with their ladders. I was lucky enough to have a younger friend, Michael Gross, who lived a few blocks east down Cienega in his family's custom-built home that still had a few rows of orange trees that ran perpendicular to the right of their house on their property. One Halloween, Michael, his sister Renee (who was my age), his older brother Bobby, and I created a haunted pathway of cardboard headstones and doomsday warning signs with spider webs and ghosts hanging from their small orange tree grove. In my mind's eye, it was spectacular; in reality, it probably looked like children had created it and something only a parent (who didn't have to take it down after their children lost interest) could appreciate.

The other local grove I remember is the one that bordered the west playing field of Charter Oak Elementary School. From what I recall, there had been reports of a man in the area who had been exposing himself to children, likely near or in local citrus groves where he could quickly hide from authorities through a maze of orange trees providing cover. It's the same way Bernie traveled after sprinting from his dead wife to his first stolen car. The chatter on the school yard about the flasher during a recess evolved into a bunch of us deciding to form a posse to catch the offender. We ran up to the chain-link fence, grabbed hold of it with our hands, some scaling the fence in a display of their superhero prowess or, as an adult who might have disapproved, like chimps in a zoo. In reality, all we could do was to squint our eyes between the links into the void of the dark and foreboding grove to see if we could spot the offender, regaling each other with what we would do to the guy if we caught him. The frenzy built as one child, then another, was sure they had seen someone—or *something*—move in the distance.

Could it be the flasher?

Would we catch the notorious Charter Oak Flasher?

Hysteria mounted. But before we could storm the fence, knock it over, and tear him limb from limb, an on-duty teacher came running over and broke up the mob. Alerted by a tattle tale—or less interestingly, spotting us hanging from the fence—she made her way over, and shut the party down.

Killjoy!

I've forgotten how fearless kids can be when merging into a vigilante party when they have no authority to do so or physical prowess to back it up, similar to their judgmental attitudes about George Reeves' suicide when they had no facts or evidence.

Although Bernie grew up in Covina when the orange was still king, he preferred to stay as far away from citrus groves as possible. Tennis and the cornet topped his interests. He had big plans and citrus ranching—or processing oranges like his grandfather once did—was not part of them. His parents doted on him, and even his two younger sisters knew Bernie was the prince in their family and soon beyond the confines of their home as well. If new residents in town weren't properly aware of Bernie's status, they soon were by reading the *Covina Argus-Citizen*.

Ads for various Finch family enterprises populated the newspaper for decades. These in turn guaranteed coverage with the paper reporting the family's every social event, from birthday parties, weddings, and vacation travels, to early 1900s challenges, like Thomas' automobile drive from Covina to Long Beach over dirt roads, and Raymond's broken arm caused by a cantankerous hand crank that kicked back when he tried to start his car. Even when a family member got the "grip" (as we now call the flu) it was duly reported.

The Finches worked hard to expand Bernie's kingdom. His career path was set at an early age as a medical doctor. But by whom? Raymond? Bernie? Marian Eva? All three? No matter the combination, Bernie was on board with the plan. Although Raymond was an optometrist, he was not a "real" doctor. He could not operate on people and hold their lives in his hands. Bernie would. He would elevate the family's status further by becoming the first medical doctor in the family. Only a career as a lawyer who later ran for public office would have carried as much cachet.

Bernie graduated a year and half early from Covina High School in June 1934, just six months after turning sixteen. He took a year off before entering nearby La Verne College (now the University of La Verne) as an undergraduate. He was as close to his family as any son could be, even staying within weekend driving distance when attending, and graduating in 1943 from the College of Medical Evangelists (now Loma Linda University). There, he met Dr. Franklin Gordon, who would eventually marry his sister Marian Louise.

Even when military service required Bernie to be stationed in North Carolina as an army surgeon, he took every opportunity to travel back to Covina with his wife Frances and their young son Tom during extended leaves to be with his parents and sisters. The Finch family admiration society was very much a two-way street.

When Bernie was discharged at the end of World War II, he began his medical practice at the Magan Clinic in Covina (which was then located at 155 W. College Street), just blocks away from the beautiful Spanish-style stucco home where Raymond, Marian, and the girls lived at 444 Cedar Drive. If Bernie so desired, he could have walked to their home for lunch by cutting through Covina Municipal Park, since the home he shared with Frances, Tom, and now baby

Sharon (with a second girl, Linda, on the way in 1948) was four miles away (1333 Bonnie Cove Avenue).

As a young boy, Bernie and Marian Louise lived with their parents in a small wooden bungalow, one of many that dotted both sides of Cottage Drive. Cottage was one block north and parallel to College Street, where Bernie was likely treated by doctors as a five year old when the Magan Clinic opened in 1923 and where he would eventually work as a doctor. The Cottage Drive home was just blocks away from Raymond's optometry office on Citrus, which was next door to Finch's Jewelers, which he co-owned with his brother. If you add in Thomas Finch's milling company and the grocery/department store across the street to this mix, you could have thrown a rock in downtown Covina, hit someone in the head during the first half of the twentieth century, and in all likelihood, that person's last name would have been Finch.

It's hard to say when Bernie's wandering eye began. Fortunately for him, the *Covina ArgusCitizen* didn't report the salacious shenanigans of the town's upstanding citizens for gossips who covered their tittering with hankies and exchanged *ahems* and *I-told-you-sos*. If the paper had covered them, Bernie's speeding and drunk driving would have been duly noted. Even so, when Bernie was stopped by local police, they did not ticket or arrest him on his way to an "emergency," wearing his white medical smock, a stethoscope in the pocket, and the smell of liquor on his breath. If the police had, the *Argus-Citizen* would have looked the other way.

The paper took in a significant portion of its revenue generated through ads paid for by the various Finch enterprises over the decades. If the paper, which ceased publication in November 1958, had survived just another eight months, it would have been interesting to see how it reported—if it reported—Barbara Finch's death and Bernie's role in it.

It's likely Bernie's extramarital affairs began even before meeting Barbara Jean Daugherty when she came to him as a patient at the Magan Clinic. Women, in a culture which gave them little value, even if they worked outside the marital home, might seek self-expression and comfort in ways their husbands could not, or would not, provide nor support. Bernie, a handsome, charming young doctor, did not go by unnoticed, particularly by women he worked with at Magan, Inter-Community Hospital, also in Covina, Monrovia Hospital in nearby Monrovia, and Lark Ellen Hospital in West Covina.

There are no published records of potential liaisons with female employees, but there would later be court reports about those he had at West Covina Medical Clinic (WCMC). It seems unlikely that Bernie's affairs just started at WCMC without a prior history at the others. Of course, he *did* co-own WCMC and possibly assumed that although Magan and the others could fire him if he were caught with a nurse or office worker, his own medical clinic could not. Whether this thought existed in Bernie's mind or not, in reality, it would prove to be the flashpoint for his eventual downfall.

Bernie would deliver Barbara's daughter Patti Dee by caesarean in 1947. He and his wife Frances moved into their Baldwin Park home at 14537 E. Rockway the following year. Was it a coincidence that the home they bought also happened to be right next door to Barbara Jean Daugherty, her husband Lyle, and daughter Patti? Not likely.

So then how *did* Bernie and Barbara maneuver his family into the neighborhood?

After the birth of Patti but before the Finches moved next door, Barbara began working for Bernie as his medical assistant at the Magan Clinic. It's probable her extended hours of going over Dr. Finch's paperwork at the clinic began to turn into a much more nefarious activity in Lyle's mind, particularly when he noticed that Bernie hadn't arrived at his home either after office hours. Did Lyle run next door to check with Frances on their spouses' whereabouts? Did he share his suspicions with her? Did she with him?

How many late nights did Barbara need to work in a week?

Lyle wasn't stupid. He'd demand that Barbara quit her job and end the affair or they would move. For Barbara, it was a very real threat that might mean moving to an even less desirable city than Baldwin Park—if there was one. Maybe it wasn't even Finch she had fallen for, but what he represented: an escape from a marriage to a man who was almost twenty years older than she, and his blue-collar job as a mechanic that guaranteed she would never be able to move up from their middle-class existence.

Barbara remembered another time, a much happier one when her family had money. She had once lived in Beverly Hills at 315 South Rodeo Drive and, even though it was in the city's "flats" and not north of Santa Monica Boulevard where the cream of the city rose to the top of the incline, her family still had a Scottish maid, Isabella, to tend to her, older brother Jack, father Walter, and mother Janett.

Then, just as quickly as the Reynolds family had attained its status, it was gone, wiped out by the Great Depression. Walter owned a shoe store in Beverly Hills that sold to wealthy clients who now tightened their purses, afraid themselves of losing status from their worthless paper fortunes. Who knew when or where it all might end? They could sacrifice and make ends meet by cutting out the custom shoes they bought from Walter. With the loss of the business and their home, the Reynolds were forced to move down a notch to lesser-scale Santa Monica and, at some point, Walter began to drink.

But Santa Monica was still a step above where Barbara's social slide would ultimately end, in the Antelope Valley in the high desert seventy miles north of Los Angeles. By then, in 1936, her parents had divorced, and Janett, who then owned and managed a dress shop, had married a local veterinarian, George Todd.

If Barbara stayed married to Lyle, they would, in all likelihood, never leave Baldwin Park. She might as well be living again in the Antelope Valley. More so, Lyle's age and blue-collar job couldn't compete with the much-younger, charming, handsome Dr. Finch. When Lyle finally confronted her about the affair, Barbara refused to end it. She *had* a job and what that didn't cover, Bernie would be more than happy to provide. Bernard Finch would put her back on the pedestal where she belonged: if not Beverly Hills, then at least West Covina in the castle he promised to build for Lady Barbara on the hilltop. Bernie assured Barbara West Covina would soon become the cultural and economic center of the Eastern San Gabriel Valley. The proposed South Hills Country Club, which would include a golf course and tennis courts, would be built just below their home. They could stroll there on a cool moonlit night for cocktails and conversation with other club members or for a warm summer night game of tennis, a game which Bernie excelled at and would teach her to play. Bernie would make Barbara his queen and together they would rule the San Gabriel Valley.

Barbara would not be denied.

On January 3, 1949 Lyle filed for divorce in Pomona Superior Court. In the six-page attached property settlement, they agreed that if Barbara ever married Bernie, Lyle would get custody of two year old Patti Dee. It was a deal she would make to escape. Frances and Bernie soon followed suit and divorced. Bernie and Barbara moved out of their respective homes, while remaining next-door neighbors and divorcees Frances and Lyle commiserated and cried on each other's shoulders until they romantically fell into each other's arms.

They would marry on October 9, 1954, almost three years after Bernie and Barbara.

Bernie and Dr. Gordon developed and built the West Covina Medical Clinic at 741 S. Orange Drive, just four miles west of the hilltop home Bernie promised to build for Barbara if all their hopes and dreams for the new facility came true.

Bernie's and Franklin's timing couldn't have been better. Subdivisions in the Eastern San Gabriel Valley were exploding out of the detritus of the Quickly Declining orange groves with new tracts of homes in Covina, West Covina, Charter Oak, La Puente, Rowland Heights, Azusa, and Baldwin Park. In 1950, the year following Barbara and Bernie's divorces, the medical clinic opened just off Garvey Avenue, which engineers were now using as the footprint to develop and build the new San Bernardino Freeway. The freeway, when finished, would be the major artery from Los Angeles through the San Gabriel Valley to San Bernardino and beyond to Palm Springs. The freeway would carry post-war baby-boom families to their new homes and the shopping centers that line its corridor and, when they're hurt, into the waiting, healing arms of Bernie and Franklin. It would be like shooting fish in a barrel. The new medical clinic couldn't miss, Bernie and Franklin told prospective backers when seeking loans for construction.

On June 25, 1950, my parents, after having met the previous year at the annual Russian Molokan picnic, were married in East Los Angeles. My father was driving trucks and trailers locally, and hauling rock and sand to build that freeway and everything else in the Los Angeles area for Azusa Rock & Sand. My mother worked at Pacific Telephone in downtown Los Angeles as a telephone operator. They initially lived in an apartment in East Los Angeles, then, in short time, bought a small two-bedroom, one-bath home at 6513 Paramount Boulevard (later re-designated 6533 Phaeton Avenue) in an unincorporated area of Los Angeles

County then known as Rivera (and after 1958, Pico Rivera). My mother soon discovered she was pregnant and asked a girlfriend at the phone company if she could recommend a doctor. She recommended Dr. Bernard Finch. My mother was pregnant, but not with me. After she suffered a "silent" miscarriage, one wherein the fetus did not develop and her body didn't discharge it nor the tissues, Dr. Finch performed a dilation and curettage, known as a D&C. The cervix is dilated to allow access to the uterus, which then has its contents removed, generally by scraping the uterine walls with a curette instrument, followed by suction. Whatever part of this procedure Dr. Finch performed on my mother, it occurred between July and October 1950. My mother told me many years later that my father insisted she not have the D&C because, in his mind, she would be having an abortion. But how can you abort a life that doesn't exist? Or one that ceased to exist? Somehow, she managed to convince him otherwise and he trusted her decision.

Since WCMC did not yet have a hospital in 1951, Dr. Finch had surgical privileges at Monrovia Hospital, which was where I was born by caesarean that August. Four months later, on December 22, Bernie and Barbara married in Las Vegas. They finally moved into their hilltop castle in West Covina when it was finished seven months later in July 1952. Frances and Lyle Daugherty married in 1954, the year Dr. Finch delivered my sister, Carol Ann Kosareff, on December 28, again at Monrovia Hospital by caesarean. All seemed to be on track with the Finch and Kosareff households—that is, until Carole Ann Tregoff came looking for a job at the WCMC.

*Carole Tregoff (on right) and her beloved
stepmother, Gladys during the first murder trial
on February 10, 1960. The two couldn't have
been closer unless they were conjoined twins.*

CHAPTER 7 – IN HER
OWN LITTLE CORNER

Carole Tregoff's life, as the public has come to know it, began behind a bougainvillea bush on July 18, 1959. She never wavered in her claim through three trials that she hid there during Bernie and Barbara's epic life and death struggle. Everything leading to her meeting Dr. Bernard Finch and everything that followed—including the notoriety, murder trials, prison, release, and her internet following (where fans trade photos and fantasize about her existence)—traced back to her bougainvillea bush alibi. Carole's life, as far as the general public is concerned, came to an end in 1969, when the thirty-two year old shed her infamous public persona after her parole from prison with a name change and disappeared, never to be heard from again.

Well, almost.

After her release, it became known by sleuthing fans (and contemporary *Los Angeles Times* readers who spotted the small article buried in the back of the paper) that Carole took a job under a new name in the Records Department at Intercommunity Hospital in Covina. Intercommunity was, and still is, located in the middle of the old Finch family haunts: their homes, businesses, and the Magan Clinic. Bernie even once had surgical privileges at Intercommunity. Carole continued working there for decades, eventually running the department until retirement. Although she legally changed her name to maintain some semblance of anonymity, employees at Intercommunity knew who she was, although she never discussed her past with them. But they soon had an option to read about it and discuss it amongst themselves when she was out of the office on vacations.

When medical doctor/amateur sleuth/author James L. Jones researched his 1992 book, *A Murder in West Covina*, he wrote Carole a letter, asking for her participation in the project. He never heard back, and according to the hospital grapevine, she was not happy about the prospect of a book detailing a period of her life she'd rather forget. If she read the book after it was published, she had good reason to dislike it for reasons other than how she was portrayed. Many events in the book, like the actions surrounding the prosecuting attorney's re-creation for reporters of Barbara's body lying on the ground in Raymond Finch's front yard and the non-existent superior court case files Jones claimed his researchers pored over for the Finch trials, are fabrications. A good eye could also spot a caption on a photo in the book incorrectly identifying *Perry Mason* producer Gail Patrick Jackson as L. Patrick Gray (in reality, the former acting director of the FBI during the Nixon Administration). Still, a less demanding reader may swallow his story whole, keep turning the pages, and read on, but Jones' paraphrasing of trial testimony crosses a line.

During research for this book, I compared courtroom dialogue in Jones' book to contemporary newspaper accounts. Jones, while generally following the sequence of events, did not follow testimony that newspapers reported. During my access to trial transcripts at the Los Angeles District Attorney's office, I was able to confirm the newspaper accounts of trial testimony conformed very closely to the trial transcripts I had in front of me. A question remained as to whether the trial transcripts were themselves transcriptions from stenotype paper tapes made by a court reporter during live testimony. If so, there could be errors on those that were then copied to the transcripts, but we may never know for sure unless the stenotype paper tapes still exist and can be compared to the transcripts. Even so, we can never prove the accuracy of the stenotype tapes.

Jones noted a disclaimer on his book's cover, calling the content "a based on fact dramatization," thereby absolving himself of any mistakes in his book due to muddying the waters mixing fact and fiction.

What else could he do in 1992?

• The police wouldn't let him look at their files if he contacted them, likely due to the department's incompetence at the time of the murder; including its not taking Barbara's calls for help seriously and officers on scene not discovering the attaché case and alpine hat;

• There were no case files in the archives of Los Angeles County Superior Court as he stated (I did locate them in the district attorney's office off-site storage facility, which took some doing to gain a very limited, non-recordable, chaperoned access);

• The internet didn't exist for additional research outside libraries;

• Jones didn't know any of the significant players who were still alive *and* they weren't talking; and

• Jones didn't live in the area at the time of the murder.

Jones did interview a few people who were alive at the time or peripherally involved with the case, but their questionable connections, age, and time passed made for unreliable memories and non-substantial material. The only person Jones interviewed who was young enough, still alive in 1992, and a key player in the story was the Finches' Swedish au pair, Marie Anne Lidholm.

Marie Anne had returned to her native Sweden years before, so Jones interviewed her over the phone and through correspondence. All other living players at the time (if Jones contacted them) including Patti Daugherty, Raymond Finch Jr., Gladys Tregoff, James Pappa, Carole Tregoff, and Dr. Bernard Finch, refused to participate. Since the book's publication, Bernie and Gladys have passed away. Carole and Jimmy are still alive and in their eighties as of this writing. In the past, writers have tried to contact Carole. It's always proven to be a dead end. Spotting and identifying her in public is still as elusive as shooting a clear photo of Sasquatch.

But it has been done.

Gary Cliser, who created the blog *The Many Faces of Carole Tregoff Pappa,* was just an infant at the time of the murder, but his parents, who lived behind her, had a ringside seat without fences blocking their view of the initial Finch-Tregoff trysts. The Clisers' backyard abutted Carole and Jimmy Pappa's at 1263 Big Dalton Avenue in La Puente. Cliser's parents told him years later that they spotted Dr. Finch arriving at the Pappas' home after Jimmy had left for work on a number of occasions. Cliser, several years after his blog had been created, met with *Los Angeles Magazine* reporter Steve Mikulan for his April 2013 article "Murder in Black and White" at the South Hills Country Club in West Covina. An older waitress working in the clubhouse overheard them discussing Carole and told Gary and Steve that Carole had her hair styled at a salon on Rowland Avenue in Covina.

Didn't sound like Carole was exactly hiding from the public in her former stomping grounds. Nor did she try and run away when Jimmy Pappa's sister ran into her in a supermarket in Covina circa 2008-09 and was told by Carole that she had "earned every gray hair on her head" (which I'm guessing is tended to at the Unique Hair Designs by Linda Evans on Rowland Avenue. It looks just like the salon where your grandmother might feel comfortable having her hair styled. For Carole, then nearing eighty, she would have been right at home.) Then again, when Mikulan wrote Carole to say he would be calling about the article he was writing—and did—she hung up as soon as he identified himself. Even Jimmy Pappa, who still carries the torch of unrequited love (as he defines it), was hung up on by Carole when he called.

Next to her father James, Carole's stepmother Gladys Tregoff was her biggest supporter during the trials. Twenty-five years later, Gladys and James were still living in the same home in South Pasadena they once shared with Carole, until James passed away in 1987. Gladys continued to live in the home until her age and infirmity required she be moved to an assisted care facility in 2000 and the home was sold. Gladys would pass away six years later.

During the trials, the house at 1230 Oak Hill Avenue was well known to reporters. When Carole was out of jail on bail, she and Gladys entertained from the front porch steps with their pronouncements and repartee on the trials. Reporters were also privy to more personal aspects of their lives—good and bad—including Carole's playing the family piano or, in the case of her rearrest, when she was dragged out of the home by court bailiffs against her will.

In less contentious times, when detectives followed Carole after the murder to keep tabs on her and parked across the street, she was happy to please and walked out with a tray of cookies for them. An Intercommunity Hospital records employee, who wished to remain anonymous, told Mikulan years later that Carole was a wonderful boss. "She was very kind, fair, and compassionate." She likely then provided milk with the cookies for the detectives.

Even still, Carole continued to maintain her anonymity outside her place of employment. Did she represent the Tregoff Estate when the home was sold in 2000? Or was Gladys still cognizant enough to sign the agreement? Or was it an estate attorney? Or could it have even been Carole under her assumed name? Outside of Carole, only the new owner, Diane Margrave, with the signature on her copy, knows. Was Margrave aware of the home's notorious past? Could she have even been a friend of Carole's?

When Gladys died, she was buried, along with her husband and Carole's father, James (who had passed in 1987), at Rose Hills Memorial Park in Whittier. In mortuary records there is contact information for the responsible burial and grave site maintenance agent. Is it under Carole's new name? Does she visit the grave sites? The mortuary, citing confidentiality, will not say.

Did Carole run a personal ad in a local paper in May 1969 upon her prison release announcing her name change as required by law for any potential creditors seeking remuneration? Or since this involved a high-profile criminal case and would have exposed her new identity, was she given a pass by the court?

Would I even recognize Carole Ann Tregoff or Carole Ann Smith or Carole Ann Jones or Carole Ann Whatever if I saw her on the street today?

Might I have passed right by her decades earlier when visiting my parents in Covina? Could she have been living nearby? A house down the street near our family home on Garsden Avenue?

Next door?

Right behind?

Or did Carole make it a habit to check out potential neighbors before any move to see if they were former Finch patients who might be able to identify her? Does she still look anything like the twenty-one year old I remember as a seven year old, standing just behind Dr. Finch, furiously writing notes in my medical file, in front of the swinging saloon-style double doors leading in and out of the brick-walled exam rooms?

Did Carole, when noticing that both our family last names ended with a double *F*, ask my mother if we were Russian? *Could we be related?*

Carole's father James was married three times during his life. His first wife, according to a 1930 US Census, was Myrtle E. Chick, whom he had married in 1929. By 1935, Myrtle was out of the picture and James had married Jeanne Gray Lewis. She gave birth to their daughter Carole Anne on December 25, 1936. The marriage was problematic and it appears Jeanne was not faithful to James. Years later, during the Finch murder trial, when he was questioned on the witness stand and asked if Carole was his daughter, he told the court, "I assume so," to which there were audible gasps and laughter from those present.

On March 1, 1943, James would marry Missouri native Gladys Lee (Martin) McNally, a divorcee. About a year later, eight year old Carole would live with her father and stepmother. Gladys, who had no children of her own, and Carole grew close and Carole came to consider Gladys her mother, rarely ever contacting Jeanne. Her life with James and Gladys was idyllic compared to the one she previously had with her birth mother and stepfather.

The following year, Carole, still living with her mother and stepfather, later told the court during her murder trial that as a little girl she would tune out the sound of Jeanne and her second husband, Fremont Albert, fighting by hiding in a closet for hours, all to support her alibi that she had hidden hours in the bougainvillea bush the night of Barbara's murder. When she later repeated this story to a reporter shortly after her sentencing in 1961, she added that on at least one occasion both of them had been drunk and Jeanne charged at Fremont with a large kitchen knife. This story, if true, and Jeanne's infidelity and mental instability, would explain why James left and Carole was miserable staying with her.

Although Jeanne made an appearance at the hearing for Carole in West Covina in support of her daughter, Carole summed up her childhood relationship with her mother, saying, "It's not that I don't love my real mother. I do. But it's possible to love someone and not respect her." It's also likely Carole picked up some of her traits from the mother she disrespected. Although she looked like an older femme fatale with her features and style of dress, Carole would later be seen as either a naïve, unsophisticated Juliet or a cunning Mata Hari with her display of tears, brave little smiles, and numerous breakdowns in court. In reality, she was *both*. "A dormant temper, stubborn willfulness, and a readiness to plunge headlong into irretrievable situations," as one reporter concluded during one of the trials.

James' marriage to Gladys was different than his to Jeanne. They would remain married through their daughter's murder trials, imprisonment, release, name change, and new life until his death in 1987. Carole would remain close to both of them until their passing. Prior to their living in South Pasadena, the Tregoffs lived in two apartments near where my father once lived in Boyle Heights. Carole, now living with her family at 2856 Camulos Place, attended Huntington Park High School three miles south. She would graduate from there in 1954, as did my mother eight years earlier when she lived with her father and her stepmother within Huntington Park city limits.

In Carole's high school graduation photo she appeared as a blonde. It's a hair color no one familiar with the Finch murder case ever saw her sport during the trials where she switched back and forth between auburn (when she was out on bail and hair dye was available) and her natural brunette (while imprisoned). Carole told reporters during the trials that her interests in high school were modeling, Latin, and interior design. She also loved swimming and water skiing.

None of them, however, would lead her to Dr. Bernard Finch.

CHAPTER 8 – JIMMY, OH
JIMMY, SILLY BOY

Carole first laid eyes on Jimmy Pappa when she was fourteen and he seventeen at a party in Alhambra. She claimed that she didn't think at all about him until she saw Jimmy the following year at a Woodrow Wilson High School gym meet in El Sereno where he was twirling his body on the rings. "He had a beautiful physique, was sure of himself, and was very much the 'Big Man on Campus," she told a *Los Angeles Mirror* reporter in 1961 just days after her sentencing.

Jimmy was ready to get hitched now that he was graduating from high school, but Carole, with more than two years left, wasn't even considering it and cooled his jets. Instead, to bide his time, Jimmy got hitched to the Marines. By the time his two-year stint would be up, he figured, Carole would be graduating from Huntington Park High School and ready for marriage. He wasn't far off the mark. Upon his discharge, Carole was finally open to considering marriage to Jimmy. Many of the girls she knew in school were getting married now that everyone was graduating. It seemed the appropriate next step for a young woman at the time, so Carole and Jimmy tied the knot in Las Vegas.

But from the start something wasn't right. Carole wasn't in love with Jimmy and began to seek male company outside her marriage. She went out with mostly older men. Astonishingly, she thought that maybe there was still a chance that as time passed she would still fall in love with Jimmy *while* carrying on on the side. Instead, reality

James "Jimmy" Pappa – July 1959. Culture model and day worker, Jimmy would soon add "ex-husband" to his resume when Carole Tregoff filed for divorce.

interceded and her relationship with Jimmy continued to veer off course. It finally landed in sibling territory. Even her nascent modeling career couldn't survive the marriage. As far as Jimmy was concerned, there was room for only one model in the family and *he* was it.

In between blue collar jobs such as gas station attendant and construction worker, egotistical Jimmy worked on his physique, constructing muscle for the body building and culture magazines he loved to pose for favored by men of both gender attractions. By 1955, they were living in their small home on Big Dalton Avenue in La Puente. Carole, bored with being a housewife in a dead-end marriage and one without even a promising career, decided a change was in order. If she couldn't fix or get out of her marital situation, at least she could change her job. She had heard about an opening for a receptionist at West Covina Medical Clinic and decided to apply. She was hired.

Her memory and ability to retain facts must have played a part in her hiring and it proved to be a significant help in her career. About three weeks after Carole was hired, she was introduced to Dr. Finch as "the new girl." Seven months later on August 1, 1956, she moved up and was hired as Finch's medical secretary. By then she had already heard the rumors about his marital problems with Barbara and knew about his sexual conquests in the female employee pool. She even knew that the team of three that she was now joining included his current squeeze, the registered nurse assigned to him. Now that Carole was as close to Finch in a working relationship as his nurse, did the thought cross her mind of usurping the nurse's in his personal life?

"Did visions of sugar plums—and Cadillacs and country clubs—dance in her head?" as Dorothy Kilgallen would later write her in column.

Nineteen year old Carole started on a three-month trial basis as Dr. Finch's medical secretary. (Her ability to keep up with his medical directions taking notes in patients' files was amazing to this seven year old.) Seven months later, she was still working for him but, she later claimed, still in a platonic working relationship. She eventually met Barbara when she came to pick him up for a tennis date. If Barbara's marriage was shaky before meeting the attractive, decade-younger Carole, her private internal reaction upon meeting the auburn-haired beauty must have been off the Richter scale. Although she was courteous and polite to Carole, Barbara still gave off a cool, icy detachment that Carole didn't soon forget.

Carole had a dream about Finch. In it, he tried to kiss her, but she resisted and pushed him away. Several weeks later, the doctors and nurses gathered in the lunch room at the clinic. One of them brought up the topic of dreams and Carole was asked about hers. Since Finch was present she had an instant flashback and blushed, and in doing so, gave the room a verbal pass. Six months later, after they had been become romantically involved, Finch hadn't forgotten about her reaction when she was questioned about her dreams. When she told him the details, he replied that she had wish fulfillment. He promised to make that dream come true.

Still, their romantic relationship started with a seemingly platonic lunch in February 1957 during office hours at the Zanzibar Restaurant in nearby Duarte. Why they drove ten miles to a restaurant better known for its attached motel than its culinary delights isn't beyond belief if you factor in a potential afternoon tryst. But Carole claimed one didn't happen. They just had lunch. Their first "real date" took place March 1, 1957, over dinner at the trendy Tiki-themed restaurant, The Luau, in Beverly Hills. "Chief Stefooma" (owner Stephen Crane, and Lana Turner's former husband) himself may have even personally delivered one of the many rounds of scorpion cocktails for two they drank before closing out the restaurant at 2 a.m. after six hours of conversation. Did they "escort" (as the menu called it) their scorpions with appetizers to soak up the booze so Bernie could drive home? Or were they "escorted" out of the restaurant by Chief Stefooma for one too many scorpions?

Probably neither, because after leaving—or being asked to leave—they continued their date by driving aimlessly around the city and ended up in the Hollywood Hills, where Finch parked his 1957 red Chrysler 300-C convertible overlooking city lights. Carole later told the *Mirror* this was the first time Finch kissed her. "It was a kiss such as I had never experienced before." she said. "A kiss of tenderness… a kiss of friendship… a kiss of love… a kiss of respect." It was also a kiss fueled by scorpion breath.

The kiss of a lifetime for Carole was soon to be the kiss off for Jimmy. When Carole finally rolled into Big Dalton Avenue at 4:15 in the morning, Jimmy demanded to know where she had been, what she had been doing, and with whom she'd been doing it. Carole was tightlipped and not forthcoming, which only made Jimmy more mad. As punishment he forced her to call Dr. Finch and tell him she wasn't coming into work that morning. Then he grabbed the receiver from her and told *Finch* that she had been out until *4:15 this morning.*

How did Finch restrain himself from laughing? Excuse himself from the phone and grab a pillow, go into another room, and cover his mouth? Did Barbara hear him cackling from her bedroom? If so, did she just pull the covers up over her head? How long did it take for Finch to recover and avoid laughing in Jimmy's face as he told him Carole could have the day, he understood; he knew a thing or two about keeping late nights. Particularly one late night very recently. Then Finch, after hanging up, likely collapsed from laughter on the living room sofa before passing out from the previous day's scorpion-fueled love hangover and into a deep sleep, snoring.

Thus began Carole's and Bernie's series of dates over the following weeks. They made sure to each have a change of clothes with them at the clinic. They worked later than anyone else so as to maintain a front of propriety. They also made sure to end their dates early for dinner, dancing, or a movie so as not to arouse suspicion and make it look like they'd been working late. It was something Bernie's ex-wife Frances knew all too well, and now karma came knocking on Barbara's door. She found herself sitting in the same boat adrift at sea that Frances had once occupied.

Soon, Bernie's and Carole's charade became too much for them to design each date like generals planning an amphibious landing. They decided to streamline the arrangement. On April 15, 1957, six weeks after their scorpion-soaked date, Finch rented a furnished apartment for him and Carole just far enough away—so they wouldn't be seen by spouses, friends or co-workers but close enough to be convenient to work and their homes—in Monterey Park, as Mr. and Mrs. George Evans.

In the 1950s, Carole and Bernie still needed to maintain propriety to keep snooping neighbors at bay spotting their comings and goings and starting tongues wagging. Possibly to convince herself of the same and/or afraid that sex would end the relationship, Carole later said that she and Bernie waited a month before consummating their relationship in the apartment. The days and nights Carole spent with Bernie in Monterey Park were the happiest of her life.

Barbara was no fool when it came to extramarital affairs. She knew the signs from personal experience. She had *been* Carole Tregoff *before* there *was* a Carole Tregoff. She now sought two things: revenge, and, even more importantly, to maintain her living status as a doctor's wife. She failed to see that both would be combustible if combined.

Barbara was her husband's personal bookkeeper and she visited the medical clinic on a regular basis. Since she had been involved with Bernie from the beginning of the center's development, construction, and opening, she also knew the employees. She may have even been involved in the initial staffing since Bernie was co-owner and may have tried to hire not only what she perceived as the most efficient, but homeliest, women she could find to control her husband's libido. A smart woman like her would always keep her eye on the prize, which was not only her husband, but the medical clinic, particularly since she was a marital beneficiary of any profits it—and the coming hospital—would generate. She remembered what happened when her father lost his shoe store in Beverly Hills. That was never going to happen to her again. She would make sure.

With her regular presence at the medical clinic keeping an eye on the business, she could not escape the looks of jealous women who were involved with her husband behind her back; nor the other women who were only too happy to get her alone in a consultation room or on the phone to rat them out. Barbara didn't need to know their names, she already knew her husband wasn't faithful. She hated that he wasn't and tried to stop Bernie in the past, but she also knew that the women he bedded were always temporary—until the next bright, shiny one came along.

Bernie was the proverbial kid in the (medical clinic) candy store. As long as she could look the other way, she could maintain her propriety, and financial and social status. She put her energy into shining as Lady Barbara Finch at the prestigious Los Angeles Tennis Club with her celebrity pals, like dancer/actress Vera-Ellen and actor/director Mark Stevens. If she didn't feel like driving the thirty minutes downtown, she could always slum down the hill from her home with the South Hills Country Club doctors, lawyers, and their wives. It's a life she had gotten used to since she married Bernie almost seven years earlier. She was not about to give it up now that they were so close to opening the hospital, with the revenue it would produce and move them further up the economic and social ladders.

How many people could say they own a hospital?

Then, suddenly and unexpectedly, Carole Tregoff entered the picture.

Barbara's world was shaken to its core. The young, attractive redhead was a threat she hadn't considered and wasn't the kind she'd had to deal with before, but what could she do? She couldn't tell anybody. But she had to do *something*. There was only one person who might be able to help: Jimmy Pappa.

Under the pretext of his helping to load Raymie's midget racer into a station wagon, Barbara called Jimmy and asked him to come up to Lark Hill Drive. Although Jimmy downplayed Carole's and Bernie's extensive time together, including a public appearance in Palm Springs, by the time he arrived back home, he had worked himself into a very foul mood.

When Carole returned home from work that night on September 10, 1958, Jimmy was in a rare rage and ready to pounce. He grabbed her and demanded to know where she had been. Just as her lips began to form an alibi, he slapped her across the face. Before Carole could respond, he told her about his conversation with Barbara. He asked her to deny the affair, but she wouldn't. They were at a stalemate.

The following day, after Jimmy had left for work, Carole called Bernie and told him she was leaving Jimmy. Bernie couldn't be happier. When Jimmy returned that evening and opened the front door, he must have initially thought he was in the wrong house. It was empty. Of everything. All of the furniture was gone, as was Carole's clothing and personal items, and more importantly, so was Carole. The next day, she filed for divorce.

A few days later, Jimmy showed up unannounced at the clinic. He found Carole and told her that he wanted to speak with both her and Dr. Finch. They hastily found Finch, and the three of them located an empty consultation room and closed the door. "I was so nervous and frightened that I remember almost nothing about what happened," she recalled three years later, after the murder trials.

She did, however, remember that Jimmy told them he knew about their relationship and wanted Finch to end it. Finch denied the affair, even continuing to do so after Jimmy told him Carole did not deny it and Barbara confirmed it. A few years later, on the witness stand, Jimmy told the court that he also told Finch he would sue him for alienation of affection. According to Jimmy, Finch responded, "If you do, I will get you for slander... I will have you working for me for free the rest of your life." For a day laborer like Jimmy, and with Finch's status, it probably appeared as a threat the doctor could make good on.

The one person no one has ever spoken or written about and who likely witnessed this messy and very public domestic confrontation and had as much status as Finch (but more respect) was Dr. Gordon. With the hospital scheduled to open the following month, what he didn't need was a public scandal that could sink the project. What he didn't see or hear passing through the walls among the three behind the closed door of the consultation room, he was likely told by not one but every employee who witnessed it. He probably called an emergency board meeting—without Bernie—to decide what to do. Franklin had put up with Bernie's shenanigans since he married Barbara. He had even told his father-in-law that he wanted to have Bernie committed, likely due to his alcoholism and womanizing. Franklin, a kind and reasonable man, made his case to the board. He had tried talking sense into Bernie in the past. But this time, Bernie had gone too far and now his sexual hijinks were playing out, not only in public for the entire staff to see, but also for patients waiting for their appointments in the lobby. It was bad for business. The new hospital was opening in a month.

It was possibly decided by the board not to terminate Bernie altogether, but to lighten his workload so to keep his name on the business—and creditors in the dark. After all, he had guaranteed the construction loans. It would be bad for business if Dr. Finch all of a sudden disappeared. But the board couldn't continue to let Finch run a daily practice which exposed him, other doctors, and the board to the legal ramifications, and physical and monetary costs resulting from malpractice suits brought by his inability to focus on medicine while involved with a married woman, and the board having to deal with whatever an enraged husband might do on the premises. It wasn't head receptionist Cricket's job to referee family feuds or call the cops if a fight broke out between Finch and a woman's husband and he kicked in the TV set in the waiting room or one of them ended up being thrown into the fireplace.

The West Covina Medical Clinic lobby was not a Western saloon!

I don't know how Dr. Gordon and the board orchestrated the change in Bernie's medical practice and the transition of his patients to other doctors. Maybe they threatened him with losing everything, including his investment. Whatever form it took, West Covina Medical Clinic families were likely notified by letter telling them that Finch was making changes in his practice and they needed to consider having another doctor on staff for their families. That is probably how my mother, in her eighth month of carrying my sister Debbie when Jimmy barged into the medical clinic, ended up having her baby delivered *not* by Dr. Finch, but by Dr. Gordon the day the hospital opened the following month, on October 21, 1958.

Sixteen months later, on the witness stand, Dr. Gordon would testify that the following month, November 1958, he had Finch sign a letter protecting the medical center from Finch's "voluntary retirement" or a divorce from Barbara. With the one-two punch of Finch's philandering and the opening of the hospital, Gordon didn't need a psychic reading tea leaves to tell him what was coming.

Nor did my mother. Dr. Gordon would be our family doctor from now on.

Steven, don't mention Dr. Finch's name in the clinic.

We would never see Dr. Finch again.

CHAPTER 9 – WHAT DO YOU CALL SPOUSAL ABUSE?

Therapy.

An article in the issue of *Time* magazine dated 50 years ago today—Sept. 25, 1964—highlights a mind-boggling study that concludes couples stay in abusive relationships because their fighting can "balance out each other's mental quirks."

Yep, seriously. "Mental quirks."

The study, which was published in the Archives of General Psychiatry, looked at thirty-seven cases of assault between couples in Massachusetts courts and found a common trend: "though reasonably hard-working and outwardly respectable, [the husbands] were in reality 'shy, sexually, ineffectual mother's boys.' The wives also fitted a pattern—'aggressive, efficient, masculine and sexually frigid.'"

Perhaps we shouldn't be surprised that 1960s scientists subscribed to such rigid gender norms wherein shy men were "mama's boys" and bold women were "frigid." But the science behind alcohol causing a role reversal in every couple, which was another element of the study, is questionable at best: "Usually the wife was boss, and her weak-willed husband was content to play the subservient role—until he had a few drinks. Then 'role alternation' would take place, and the husband would insist belligerently upon his conjugal rights." (By "insisting on conjugal rights" the writer does probably mean rape.)

What's most shocking is that doctors believed that a man beating his wife under these circumstances was actually a good thing. They called it "violent, temporary therapy": "The periods of violent behavior by the husband," the doctors observed, "served to release him momentarily from his anxiety about his ineffectiveness as a man, while giving his wife apparent masochistic gratification and helping probably to deal with the guilt arising from the intense hostility expressed in her controlling, castrating behavior.'"[4]

This, then, was the contemporary midcentury view that many therapists shared, qualifying spousal abuse. It was also how the public viewed men, women, marital relations, and their rigid, fixed places in the culture. "Sexually frigid" is also how Dr. Finch would describe Barbara in court as part of his murder defense. He also conveniently failed to speak of his alcoholism and the greater physical abuse Barbara suffered at his hands that might have put her in that state of mind, if indeed she was.

In January 1959, the same month Carole's divorce was finalized from Jimmy, Barbara met with divorce attorney Joseph T. Forno in Beverly Hills. She decided that the status of being Lady Barbara Finch was finally too much to bear due to his verbal and physical abuse. She told Forno she'd had enough. In what would later prove prescient, Barbara also told Forno that if Bernie came after her again, she planned to "kick off her high heels" and run down the driveway to her father-in-law's home.

The West Covina Hospital had finally opened and was on track to be a success. As Barbara saw it, the Finches and Gordons no longer needed construction loans and although they still had to finish paying off the ones they had, the hospital would soon start generating profits. Now was the

4. https://time.com/3426225/domestic-violence-therapy/

time to cut Bernie loose. Divorce didn't mean she would lose everything. In fact, she might not lose *anything*. At the time, California didn't have no-fault divorce. Everything was not automatically split 50/50. If Barbara could prove Bernie had not been faithful, she was not only likely to win big, but likely win *everything*: the hilltop home, the cars, the boat, investments, cash, and, the biggest prize of all, co-ownership of the West Covina Medical Clinic, labs, and hospital. She wouldn't be the *wife* of a hospital owner; she would *be* the owner. It all added up to about $750,000 (in 2020, $6.7 million).

Forno suggested that Barbara hire a private investigator to follow Bernie and Carole to get the goods on them when they left their new Monterey Park apartment (a second, much nicer one with "wall-to-wall carpeting"). He referred her to private investigator William S. Lewis, whom she told she would probably be dead by Christmas due to her husband's physical abuse. Lewis hired a second tier of investigators to follow Bernie and Carole when they left their love nest, but when the two spotted their pursuers, the couple sped off, foiling any attempt to catch them in *flagrante dilicto*.

Unfortunately for Bernie and Carole, their apartment was another matter. Lewis successfully bugged the place, likely when they were out trying to shake the two men tailing them while others posing as repairmen installed recording equipment. The audio Lewis got from Bernie's and Carole's mundane activities, such as cooking and playing records to their grindhouse heavy petting and sexual gymnastics, was recorded on tapes that guaranteed a schoolmarm's blushing in the jury box if they ended up in divorce court. Although Barbara's death prevented their intended use, they would later be used in her murder investigation and subsequently entered as evidence during the trials.

Lewis also suggested that Barbara hire a bodyguard, but apparently the thought of someone tailing *her* was too much to swallow. She was trying to entrap Bernie, *not* herself. She didn't want a witness to her comings and goings. Besides, she rarely saw Bernie now that he'd moved out. And when she knew he was coming to see Raymie or for some other reason he needed to be in the home, she made herself scarce, either playing doubles at the Los Angeles Tennis Club or staying with a friend for a few days. She decided against hiring a bodyguard and due to the lack of incriminating results trying to entrap Bernie and Carole to get evidence of his adultery (apart from the tapes) and the mounting cost, she dropped the investigation. However, she did not stop considering the prospect of divorce, with Forno continuing to maintain an open file.

On May 15, an enraged Bernie arrived at the Lark Hill Drive home and, with no one else there other than Barbara, he broke into the house through a second bedroom door, which led outside. A violent struggle ensued in the bedroom between them. He choked and threatened to kill her. He knocked her down so she hit her head against a nightstand, cutting it just above the left eye. He then tried to put clothes on Barbara and get her into the Chrysler.

It's not clear whether Finch intended to shove the car (with Barbara in it) over the embankment next to the garage (as Marie Anne later told the court) or whether Finch had a change of heart at the last minute and was just trying to get a hysterical Barbara medical attention after her accident (as he will later claim), but in either event, he ended up stitching the wound above her eye at the clinic. In the aftermath over the next few days, there would be three witnesses to Barbara's physical abuse: Finch, au pair Marie Anne, divorce attorney Joseph Forno, and Barbara's friend Marca Helfrich, whom she met the previous year in Palm Springs at a tennis match.

The next Sunday, Marie Anne tells the court at the first trial, Barbara, sobbing, a bandage over her left eye, called her into her bedroom and showed her the bloodied sheets. "My husband tried to kill me last night... he was going to push the car over a cliff and the car would explode." The so-called murder kit found after her death would lend credence to this scenario, since it appeared that the rope and Seconal were meant to neutralize her, allowing Bernie to place Barbara in the driver's seat of the Chrysler. When the car was pushed over the cliff with the engine running in gear, her death would look like an accident. The 300-C, like many Chrysler models from the period, had a push-button automatic transmission panel on the left side of the steering wheel. One didn't need to be in the car to put it in gear.

Where did Finch come up with this crazy scheme?

Did Carole see it in a movie? Could she have seen the 1953 film *Angel Face,* wherein Jean Simmons tampers with the family car and causes her stepmother to drive off a cliff fronting their hillside home? Did Carole suggest this scenario as a way out of their boondoggle with Barbara? If so, they weren't the only ones who may have seen the film.

The day after Finch's ill-fated plan on July 18 to send Barbara in the Chrysler over the ravine next to their home, John Robert Briggs of Pacific Palisades managed to send not only his wife but also his mother-in-law into a gorge at the top of Rustic Canyon in Santa Monica. Fortunately for the women, Briggs' wife Norma escaped from the 1958 Mercury (which also conveniently had a push button-controlled transmission) after it plunged over the edge. Briggs ran down to the car and pushed it, managing to send it further down the ravine with his mother-in-law Mary Nilson still inside. Mrs. Nilson was thrown from the moving car but miraculously managed to cling onto a bush until help arrived.

Pushing the Chrysler over the cliff appears to have been more of a threat from Finch if Barbara were to call the police. Marie Anne told the court that if Barbara had called the police, Bernie told her he knew someone in Las Vegas he could hire to kill her (although, in reality, the plan he and Carole were hatching was not that far along. At this time it was likely just Finch's unfiltered verbal wish.). According

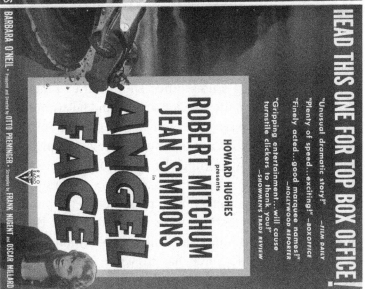

Angel Face (RKO, 1953) – In the movie Jean Simmons manages to send her hated stepmother in the family car over the cliff near their home, but unbeknownst to Simmons, at the last minute her beloved father decides to hitch a ride with his wife.

to Marie Anne, Barbara stayed in her room for several days to decompress and do some thinking. She then packed some clothing and left, telling Marie Anne beforehand that she was staying with two girlfriends in Hollywood and would call periodically to check on things at home. Barbara also told Marie Anne she was filing for divorce.

Marca Helfrich, one of the two roommates Barbara stayed with, told the court about seeing the bandaged wound over her left eye. Marca asked Barbara wasn't she afraid to let Bernie stitch her, but Barbara was more afraid if she said no. A week or two later, Barbara returned home to pick up more clothing and left a phone number for Marie Anne. Bernie asked Marie Anne about his wife's whereabouts but she didn't know. Barbara was out of the house for about three weeks and the day she returned, Bernie moved out, taking the red Chrysler and leaving the new white 1959 Cadillac, which he bought as a gift in an attempt, he will later tell the court, to placate her as part of their "armistice agreement" (because it happened on November 11).

Barbara visited Forno's office shortly after Finch beat her. She showed him the stitched wound and he arranged for photographs to be made of her injury. The photographs were entered as evidence during the murder trials and played an important part in supporting the prosecution's claim that Finch was a violent man with a bad temper, contrary to the tranquil face the charming doctor presented to the public.

Whatever his intentions were the day he beat Barbara, three days later, Bernie was still without money. If his original plan was to force her to write him a check, it backfired when he beat her. He was even more desperate for cash. On May 18, he forged a check for three thousand dollars by tracing Barbara's signature. The bank cashed it without questioning its authenticity. The bank manager and the accounts manager later tripped over their tongues trying to explain why they gave Finch the money; his defense attorney Grant Cooper presented a series of canceled checks with Barbara's signature, along with a handwriting expert, to try to prove she had signed the forged check and not Finch. Why would Finch take such risk forging a check? The amount was too high to cover an apartment for Carole. It can only be assumed he and Carole were planning to get rid of Barbara permanently by hiring someone and needed the money to do it.

On May 21, Barbara filed for divorce, charging Finch with extreme physical and mental cruelty, including nearly choking her to death. She sought control of all community assets pending a settlement, including their estate, valued at approximately $750,000 (in 2020, $6.7 million). "The doctor will bitterly protest this action at every turn," her filing stated. It would turn out to be an understatement. The following night, at 9 p.m., while she was still away from the home, Bernie, Marie Anne, and the children were watching television. There was a knock on the door. Finch answered it and was asked if he was Dr. Raymond Bernard Finch, to which he replied affirmatively.

He was served divorce papers.

On June 11, Barbara was awarded control of the Finch finances pending her and Bernie's appearance in conciliation court on July 23. After the meeting with Finch in court, Barbara told Forno that Finch's interest in wanting to reunite was only a trick so he could get back into the house to kill her. Two weeks later, Bernie got his chance. He burst into their home again, only this time there was an audience: Marie Anne and Raymie. He threatened to kill Barbara, locked the doors to the bedroom so that Marie Anne and Raymie couldn't enter, and beat her again. Barbara yelled out for Marie Anne to call the police as she and Finch moved their battle out of the bedroom and around the house.

"I'm not going to let you push me around and throw me down to the floor," Marie Anne overheard Barbara tell Bernie, as she called police.

"What do you mean, Barbara?" Finch feigned innocence. By the time Officer Kenneth D. Forrester arrived on scene, Bernie left the home. But a short time later, he called the house and asked Forrester if he could see any bruises or cuts on Barbara. Forrester did not and with the history of domestic disputes West Covina Police had answered at the Finch home in the past, it likely appeared to the all-male police department that Barbara was just another hysterical, wealthy woman complaining about her husband. *Maybe she didn't get the diamond ring he promised to buy her and this is her way of acting out.*

Finch supported this male chauvinism at the murder trial, stating he had only been at the home to switch cars again, this time his red Chrysler convertible for her white Cadillac sedan. He conveniently failed to add that he also transferred the leather attaché case from the Chrysler to the Cadillac (and a shotgun, which soon-to-be-hired conman/"killer" Jack Cody later claimed he saw in the trunk). Finch's explanation at the trial about this visit was that he started to use his key to open the door to the master bedroom from the outside when Barbara opened the door from the inside. (Marie Anne told the court that Barbara's father had installed safety chains on all the home's doors seven to ten days earlier.) Finch told Barbara he wanted to switch cars and needed the keys to the Cadillac, but she refused. She told him the keys were in the car, then fled from the room, down the hall, calling for Marie Anne to call the police. Later, in court, Finch would mention nothing of the beating Marie Anne described.

Fortuitously for the trials, Barbara called Forno after the altercation. At the first trial, he told the court that Barbara told him on June 25, three weeks before her death, that Bernie would try to get her in the car to take her out to the desert or up into the mountains to kill her and make it look like an accident. That if Bernie attempted to force her into the car, Barbara told Forno, she would bolt and run down the driveway or out of the home to her in-laws to escape.

Barbara was not going anywhere with Bernard Finch in an automobile.

Barbara saw a doctor that day who documented her bruises and swollen back. Two months after the first trial began, the *Nevada State Journal* reported that Forno told the court that Finch hit Barbara with a gun. Whether or not Finch intended to kill Barbara earlier than July 18, her fear about him was very real.

While she stayed with Marca and her roommate in the Hollywood Hills, Marca asked Barbara about a birthday celebration for her in mid-August. "It would be fine if I live until then," she responded. When Christmas plans were discussed on another occasion, Barbara replied, "We'd better hope for Thanksgiving... I don't expect to be alive for Christmas." While these remarks were objected to by the defense as hearsay and only allowed by the court to show Barbara's mental state at the time, Marca's testimony about what Barbara said about the gun Bernie kept in their home, and its disappearance, couldn't be so easily dismissed because it turned out to be true. "Well, I'm really in for it now," Barbara told Marca. "The gun is gone."

Television and film actor/director Mark Stevens, who had befriended the Finches at the Los Angeles Tennis Club, would also later testify for the prosecution. About a week before her death, Barbara confided to him that she feared for her life. He asked if she had a weapon; she said no. He suggested she get a gun and she told Stevens she didn't know how to use one and was afraid of them. He went to the Chrysler, opened the trunk, pulled out the tire iron and gave it to her. "I told her if Dr. Finch came near her to say 'hello' and hit him in the face," Stevens told the court. Stevens, who performed multiple beat downs on actors in *films noir*, placed the tire iron in the back seat of her car, on the floor. It was later found under Barbara's bed by police after she was dead.

Bernie knew he could end up losing everything in a divorce. For that reason alone he didn't want one, but he also didn't want to stay married to Barbara. He had Carole in his life. She also needed to avoid being served a subpoena as the co-respondent in Barbara's divorce petition and getting out of town looked like a good idea to prevent that. She quit her job as Bernie's medical assistant in May. As she and Bernie packed their belongings from their Monterey Park apartment, they, according to later court testimony, discussed the possibility of hiring someone to follow Barbara and get proof of an affair. Carole had a childhood friend, Donald Williams, who lived in Las Vegas, and she told Bernie that he might know someone who could help. She moved in with Williams, his older brother James, and their grandmother, Belle Morris. To support herself, she took a job in the Copa Lounge at the Sands Hotel as a cocktail waitress. About a week and a half before Barbara's murder, Bernie rented an apartment in the city for his "fiancée."

If Bernie could stall Barbara until he figured his way out of the divorce and the marital financial mess, then he might be able to hang onto his fortune—or, at the very least, most of it. He went to the divorce hearing on June 11, where Barbara was awarded control of their financials. Although angered by this action, he agreed to a hearing in conciliation court on July 23, but only, according to his claims at trial, to stall for time until he could get evidence of an affair from the investigator he'd hired to follow her. He just needed to avoid any process server with papers that would force him into court in Los Angeles. Las Vegas would be a good place to hide with Carole on the weekends. She could stay with him at the Tropicana when he was in town.

During the week, he clandestinely stayed at a long-term motel/apartment complex in West Covina, at 115 N. Walnuthaven Drive, a short distance from the medical center. Having a reduced medical practice had the unexpected benefit of preventing someone from serving him a subpoena.

If Barbara and the process server didn't know his hours at the medical center, they were less likely to catch him. Staying in the apartment motel also gave him the ability to keep a stealthy eye on their home, cars, finances, and her comings and goings to get any evidence of an affair she might be engaged in, all from a safe distance.

But as the days passed, his patience with the lack of results started to eat at his psyche. And then there was the thing that really got under his skin: Barbara's control of *his* personal finances. On July 1, she filed an Order of Temporary Support, which included her attorney's fees, court costs, and alimony. Bernie did not respond and a week later, on July 7, Barbara filed contempt charges, which he avoided being served. A date had been previously set for conciliation court on July 23 to negotiate the Finch marriage and come to a resolution or move forward with the divorce, but dealing with the contempt charge now came first. If Bernie could only be served.

Since they'd been married, Bernie kept his finances to himself. Barbara had no idea of what he truly made nor the real value of his holdings and investments. When filing for divorce, she figured it was somewhere from five hundred thousand to one million dollars, so she and Forno compromised and settled on seven hundred and fifty thousand dollars.

What did Bernie actually own?

Since Barbara had been granted control of the Finch financials, West Covina Medical Center turned over Finch's salary and income generated by the various corporate holdings, including the medical clinic, hospital, and labs, to Barbara, for accounting purposes. She deposited his doctor's salary and other income into their joint bank account. Due to the court order, Bernie could not withdraw or transfer money without Barbara's express approval. She also now paid the household and his personal bills, which included alimony payments to Frances. Bernie was also beholden to

Barbara for any pocket change she deemed suitable. And that included any funds he needed for his Las Vegas plans, which he couldn't exactly tell her about.

Bernie must have felt like a child waiting for his allowance, dependent on whether his mother approves of how well he raked the leaves.

Bernie wasn't a child!

Bernie Finch was King of the San Gabriel Valley!

And his queen had just pulled a palace coup she's going to regret.

CHAPTER 10 – VIVA LAS VEGAS, PART II

Bernie and Carole weren't professional killers. They weren't even professional crooks. They didn't have the street smarts gained from lifetimes of being on the wrong side of the law, so they were going to need help in dealing with the headstrong Barbara. The first person Carole turned to was the only one she knew and could trust in Las Vegas, her childhood friend, Donald Williams. When Carole's parents separated and before she went to live with James and Gladys, she stayed with Don, his older brother James (who, according to Finch, was a surrogate father to Carole), and their grandmother, Belle Morris. She moved in with them again on May 26, 1959.

Don testified that Carole questioned him not only about shady characters in Las Vegas, but the degree of their criminality. She confided that because of Mrs. Finch's "baseless accusations of beatings" and "objectionable activities," Carole and Bernie wanted to hire a man to "do away" with Barbara (although Carole later claimed on the witness stand it was only to seduce her to get evidence in the divorce case). "I will be quite happy when Mrs. Finch is permanently out of the picture," Don remembered Carole telling him. He was all too eager to help. He didn't personally know someone with the capabilities they were looking for but knew someone who might. Richard Keachie was a fellow classmate at the University of Nevada. Don spoke with Keachie and set up a meeting for Don and Carole at Foxy's Restaurant near campus with a man by the name of John Patrick Cody.

Jack Cody, twenty-nine, was a petty crook whose police record dated back to 1946 when at sixteen he served time at the state reformatory at Red Wing in Minnesota. His record included arrests for drunken and disorderly conduct, suspicion of robbery, assault and battery, reckless driving, and being AWOL from the army. In 1958, Cody passed a bad check and was sentenced to a year in the Hennepin County Workhouse in Minneapolis. He decided to take an unscheduled vacation and was on the lam when Carole and Don met him. To get by in Las Vegas, Cody had been working off and on—but mostly off—as a gambler's shill, and spent more time living off the many girlfriends he loved to boast about. In certain photos, Cody might be considered handsome; in others, someone who would not be beyond reaching into your pocket when your head was turned. Cody was a dark, wavy-haired, shark-tooth suited con artist and would tell someone whatever they wanted to hear to get whatever he wanted, which was usually their money.

At Foxy's, Cody presented himself to Don and Carole as a ladies man with unparalleled powers of seduction. He hinted at a dark side but did not elaborate to hold their interest. He dangled just enough tantalizing tidbits to hook Carole within ten minutes, then left, knowing she'd be back for more. After Cody was gone, Carole questioned Don about his character and any criminal activities he may have been involved in. Getting nowhere with Don, she finally got to the point: was he a murderer *or* a thief? Don didn't have a good fix on him, but Carole was intrigued enough to take a dip again in the Cody pool. It's just what he wanted her to do.

The following day, Carole and Don picked up Cody and dropped Don off at his car, which had a flat tire. After it was repaired, Don saw them a few hours later at the university restaurant. Since Don was not at the meeting with Carole and Cody, Cody would be the prosecution's sole witness as to what occurred. He and Carole discussed his being hired to murder Barbara, then negotiated and settled on a price. The murder was to appear like a robbery and it was to take place on the Fourth of July weekend when Finch would be at a tennis tournament in La Jolla and Carole at work in Las Vegas, to give them alibis. Don joined them after their meeting to give Cody a ride to the airport. Cody got out of the car, went into the terminal, made a flight reservation, and returned to Carole and Don, who were waiting for him in the car.

The next time Carole met with Cody, Bernie accompanied her; both believed, they later told the court, Cody was a private investigator. They met briefly with him in his motel room so Finch could size him up and, deciding Cody would do, they set a time for that afternoon to meet at the Sands to finalize their plans. In between the meetings, Finch rented the apartment for Carole.

The Fourth of July weekend passed and, unfortunately for Bernie and Carole, Barbara Finch was still very much alive when it was over. Finch met Cody in Las Vegas and demanded answers, but in court he told a version of what he believed occurred but did not include the murder plan. Finch stated that Cody told him he tailed Barbara over the weekend; she played tennis twice and later had dinner dates with her tennis companion, who dropped her off both times at the Hollywood Hotel Apartments. Finch pressed for more information and Cody deflected, telling Finch that their deal was for him to follow her for thirty days and he'd hand in a report. He wasn't going to give Finch any more information until then. If Cody couldn't catch Barbara in *flagrante dilecto*, according to Finch, Cody would seduce her himself. Finch was skeptical that Cody could pull it off, knowing the immense difference in social standing between the two. So Cody claimed he could pick up any woman and to prove

Finch-Tregoff co conspirator, conman and crook,
Jack Cody appears as a witness for the prosecution
at the first trial on January 19, 1960.

it, bet Finch a hundred dollars he could bed any woman he set his mind on within twenty-four hours. Finch passed, but relied on Cody's confident nature to achieve results, no matter how Barbara was seduced. Cody and Finch spent five hours in the Sands with Cody drinking but not getting drunk. They were joined by Carole after she got off work at 6 p.m. According to Finch, after a cocktail party they attended that evening, he and Carole drove Cody to McCarran Airport and bought him a second ticket.

Carole ran into Don and told him she and Finch dropped Cody off at the airport. Don found it odd because he saw Cody that night at the Hacienda Hotel. Cody, having also seen Don, knew that he likely told Carole, and went to her apartment the next morning for damage control. He told Bernie and Carole that everything was all right; he called his partner in Los Angeles and *he* was tailing Barbara. Before too many questions could be asked, he left. The next evening, on July 11, Finch and Carole picked up groceries at a market to have dinner with friends. They also purchased thirty feet of clothesline, which wasn't on the grocery list, allegedly to tie down his boat. The following day, as Finch and Carole moved her clothing to the new apartment, they saw Don at his home, where Carole had been staying. Don saw Cody again the previous night, which confirmed that Cody stiffed Bernie and Carole once again. They drove to Los Angeles.

According to Finch, the next day, July 13, he waited for Barbara to arrive at their home in West Covina. He approached the car but she refused to speak with him through the closed window, and backed the car down the driveway. On July 15, he waited again, this time at the Los Angeles Tennis Club, watching her from behind a fence as she played a game. One of her balls rolled nearby and as she retrieved it, he implored her to speak to him, but she again refused.

Cody's story differs drastically from Finch's about the Fourth of July weekend. Cody testified that Carole gave him money, hand-drawn maps of both the Finch home and Marca Helfrich's Hollywood Hills apartment building (where Barbara might also be staying), and a photo of her. He took the money and made his way to Los Angeles. He did not murder Barbara, but spent the weekend with a girlfriend, though later telling Carole the job was done.

"Are you sure you didn't talk to Mrs. Finch and she gave you a better deal?" she nervously questioned him.

"No, I didn't talk to Mrs. Finch. I just shot her!" which prompted the courtroom to erupt in laughter.

Carole, happy and smiling, called Finch to tell him, but Finch was not as quick to rely on Cody's word. He double-checked by calling his home; Barbara answered the phone.

Carole brought Finch to meet Cody in his motel room. Cody again told them he did the job, to which Finch replied that he just got off the phone with his wife and she was still very much alive. "That can't be, I shot her!"

Cody explained to them that he went to the apartment where Barbara was staying with a friend, shot a woman in the left side of her chest, put the body in the trunk of a 1951 Plymouth, and parked it behind a school.

Finch assumed he had killed Marca and told him it's a "tragic mistake." He told Cody to "go back and do it right," which caused the courtroom to erupt in laughter. Finch wanted to know how much it would cost to get him to go back and do it right. "Tell her this is for Bernie!" Finch allegedly told Cody to say to Barbara before snuffing her life out.

Cody still tried to prevent Finch from killing his wife, telling him to just let her have whatever she wanted; that if Finch truly loved Carole, they could move up to a mountain top and live off the land. The three of them then went for drinks with another couple. When Cody got on a plane to Los Angeles a second time to kill Barbara, he was very drunk. He sobered up and realized he was ninety dollars richer (Finch having stuffed cash in his pocket to complete the job). He returned to Las Vegas and met with Carole to attempt to dissuade her from killing Barbara.

She responded, "No, Jack, I've made up my mind. If you don't do it, Dr. Finch will, and if he doesn't, I will."

CHAPTER 11 – A MEDICAL INTERMISSION

During the murder investigation, it was revealed that Dr. Finch had a history of performing needless surgeries. He had also been involved directly or indirectly (through his association with other doctors at West Covina Medical Center) with eleven malpractice lawsuits, two following the deaths of children. According to James Jones, Finch was known for performing unnecessary nephropexies, a procedure involving suturing a loose kidney (that drops when a person stands up) to allegedly prevent back pain. According to Jones' anonymous source, Finch performed "dozens a month" while he was at Intercommunity Hospital in Covina. Finch was taken to task by hospital administrators and resigned shortly thereafter.

Finch, like many doctors at the time, also performed what were later considered unnecessary caesareans to deliver babies. My mother gave birth to me and my oldest sister through this procedure performed by Finch. Were my mother's caesareans necessary? Finch told her they were; so did Dr. Gordon when he performed the last two, after Finch was relieved of this duty, for a total of four.

I still have the roots to my tonsils from a botched tonsillectomy Dr. Finch performed when I was two. I had suffered sinus and breathing problems as an infant—and still do—and Finch told my parents it was probably due to the moisture from the Rio Hondo River near where we lived in Rivera. Taking out my tonsils would get rid of, or at least reduce, the congestion I was suffering. It didn't work. I continued to suffer with blocked sinuses growing up and into adulthood, especially at night, and still do when it's cold or when the wind blows allergens up my nose. A deviated septum prevents me from getting all of the oxygen I need to breathe while sleeping, causing me to snore. A timely blood test several years ago found a thickening of my red blood cells, which could have proven fatal, if not for the CPAP machine I was prescribed and use to this day.

There were more serious, even deadly, problems with other children. Finch diagnosed appendicitis in an eight-year-old girl and told her parents to take her to nearby Lark Ellen Hospital, where he had surgical privileges, for an appendectomy. While her parents waited six and a half hours for him to arrive, the girl's appendix burst. After surgery and her release from the hospital, her wound later ruptured at home. Despite the agony the girl and the parents went through, she managed to live. Other children were not so lucky.

A five-year-old boy was treated for a cut on his finger at West Covina Medical Clinic, not once but several times. He was never given a tetanus shot and soon began to develop signs of lockjaw. He was rushed to Los Angeles County General Hospital, where he later died. On another occasion, a boy swallowed oven cleaner and was given the wrong antidote.

In all three instances, the grieving parents sued and were awarded monetary judgments.

Carole Tregoff's former husband Jimmy Pappa also had a personal story about a Finchbotched medical procedure. On July 7, 1959, he sued Finch and three other doctors at the WCMC for surgery to remove a growth behind his knee, which resulted in nerve damage. He won a settlement.

All of this begs the question: How medically competent was Dr. Bernard Finch?

Should he have ever been licensed?

Was Finch's career in medicine just an avenue to even more riches?

CHAPTER 12 – THE MURDER

The day before she was murdered, Barbara called her friend, Minnette Haber, who lived in Palm Springs. Minnette was friends with both Finches and would later tell the court about the weekend Barbara and Bernie were staying with her and her husband to water ski at Salton Sea. Bernie called Carole, who was conveniently staying in Palm Springs that weekend, from Minnette's home and invited her to go along. He also disparagingly referred to Barbara that weekend as his "black bunny." When Carole arrived, she sat up front with Bernie in the car while a humiliated Barbara sat in the back with Minnette to share an awkward drive to the lake.

Now Barbara was calling Minnette to see if she could stay with her for a few days. Barbara was worried about Bernie. She had him served with a contempt of court filing and he told her to drop the charge within twenty-four hours or she would suffer consequences. If Barbara knew what those might be, she didn't tell Minnette, but it's likely both women knew exactly what Finch meant: at least another beat down. Minnette told Barbara she could stay with her, but the air conditioning in the guest room was not working properly and the temperature in Palm Springs was reaching one hundred and twenty degrees. Barbara said she'd think about it and get back to her.

She never did.

The following day, Barbara left her Lark Hill Drive home in the Chrysler and headed for a cooler clime in downtown Los Angeles. She had a doubles date at the Los Angeles

Tennis Club. After the game, her foursome had cocktails in the lounge.

Las Vegas, 6 p.m. Carole had just gotten off work when Bernie picked her up, with a change of clothes, in her white and bronze 1955 DeSoto convertible. He also had the leather attaché case in the trunk and was flagrantly carrying illegal syringes and narcotics across state lines. No other luggage was present because the trip was meant to be a short one. They would execute their plan and return to Las Vegas early the next morning. They took turns driving the five hours to West Covina, with Bernie pulling into the South Hills Country Club parking lot below his hilltop home around 11 p.m.

There's no record of what Bernie and Carole talked about during the long drive. No one bothered to ask during the trials, probably because the answers would have been selfincriminating. But it's not hard to guess what they might have chatted about, knowing they were making the drive to murder Barbara.

The first thing they likely discussed was to make sure they were on the same page about the role each would play in the plan. The murder that *does* take place is not the one they had intended, nor the one in mind as a backup. The murder Bernie and Carole *planned* was the one Barbara told Marie Anne that Finch had intended all along: they would incapacitate her, tie her up to sedate and kill her, then place her body in the Chrysler's driver's seat, and send the car over the ravine alongside the Finch garage to make it look like she overshot the driveway because she was loaded on Seconal. The Seconal they would give Barbara would render her unconscious; a second shot with an air bubble would kill her before the cruise into the ravine, and would guarantee her death was recorded as an accident. This was how Finch and Carole planned to murder Barbara.

The contents of the attaché case back this up. What's not exactly clear is the role that Carole would play. Was she to act as Finch's assistant as she had done on a daily basis at the medical clinic and just hand him the items? Or was she going to tie Barbara up as Finch held her down, then administer the injections? *Or* was she to play the more active role of nurse and give Barbara the Seconal as Finch held her down, prior to him injecting her with the air bubble? The latter seems likely, but only the two of them ever knew.

What else might they have discussed?

On the bright side, they must have looked forward to their lives together after Barbara was dead. It was likely that after a period apart, they would get married in Las Vegas and the third Mrs. Finch would move into the hilltop home on Lark Hill Drive. Carole didn't care for Bernie's institutional design, although she likely wouldn't admit it. Instead, she'd probably suggest that her interior design skills might come into play as a trial run for her potentially opening a business. Now that they were going to make a fresh start, the house should also have one as well. She might have gone so far as suggesting the contemporary popular color scheme of rose and black to show that she had already done some serious thinking on the matter.

Maybe they could even buy a second weekend home in Palm Springs. Bernie loved to play tennis there and it was close enough to Salton Sea that he and Carole could regularly go water skiing with Bernie towing her in his boat. They could even rent a mooring space. They wouldn't have to tow the boat back and forth again on its trailer!

Then there was Raymie. What to do about Raymie? Patti would obviously go back and live with her father and Frances, but Raymie was another matter. Carole really didn't want to have to face raising a small boy whose mother she had killed (she wouldn't say this out loud because it sounded vulgar and might give her pause about what she was about to do that evening). Maybe Raymie might be happier staying with people he knew and who loved him, like one of his aunts, Marian Louise or Jane, or maybe even his Uncle Jack on his mother's side. If Raymie lived with Jane, he might attend Charter Oak Elementary School, which was just a block away from her home, a short distance down Bonnie Cove Avenue.

Bonnie Cove?

Isn't that where you once lived, Bernie?

Maybe Bernie suggested that Raymie could live with *them* and they'd keep Marie Anne on to take care of him. Carole would have time to do the things she wanted. Maybe model, maybe even start that interior design business. If the idea of Raymie living with them came up, it's likely Carole didn't respond or at least tabled the thought for later. If Raymie lived with Bernie and Carole, she would not only have to face the child whose mother she had help kill, but also Barbara's young confidante and trusted employee. Marie Anne might prove to be suspicious and problematic down the road. Would Bernie and Carole have to take her out at some later date? What might authorities say then with two deaths swirling over their Lark Hill love nest?

Besides, Carole didn't like children. She never wanted any. She wanted to be Bernie's baby and, she assumed, he hers. There was only room in their relationship, as she saw it, for the two of them.

Bernie would miss the Chrysler. People who saw it loved the car (and by extension, him, for owning it), including Jimmy Pappa, who Bernie let drive it to get the overdeveloped "school boy" out of the Pappa home so he could spend some alone time with "mama" Carole. Maybe Bernie and Carole could place Barbara's body in Carole's DeSoto and push *it* over the cliff, claiming a drugged and disoriented Barbara ran out of the garage after raging at Bernie and got into the wrong car… Nah, that was too far-fetched, and besides, Barbara would never be caught in a car like Carole's DeSoto. It was too *déclassé* for her. Bernie and

Carole laughed at the thought, warmed by their love and the plan to kill his wife that would launch their new life.

Dreams and suppositions aside, Finch and Carole *will* tell the court they were going to his home to convince Barbara to get a divorce. The question they do not answer but one the jury was tasked with during the prosecution's closing: wouldn't Carole's presence at the Finch home work against her and Bernie getting Barbara to agree to a quickie divorce? Why did they think Barbara would even agree to one, let alone consider it? She had everything in the divorce suit going in *her* favor.

As the DeSoto of Death descended into the Cajon Pass that evening, and after cocktails at the tennis club, Barbara's party had dinner at Kelly's Steakhouse on Santa Monica Boulevard. She started for home a little after 11 p.m. and had no idea that a hot, dry, deadly Santa Ana wind had blown in from Las Vegas headed for her front lawn.

At the same time Barbara left the restaurant, Bernie and Carole pulled into the South Hills Country Club parking lot. Finch had Carole wait in the car. He walked up his driveway first to surveil the premises. Seeing no activity in the area, he turned off a floodlight on the property by yanking the power cord out of its outlet. He then walked over to his father's driveway below for a clear sightline to Carole and waved for her to come up. She brought the attaché case with her. The two of them later claimed they passed the time waiting for Barbara by playing with Frosty, the family's Samoyed.

But why would they expose themselves to someone potentially coming out of the Finch home—a neighbor out for a walk, or even Raymond if he stepped outside his home on the other side of the private driveway? In all likelihood, Finch and Carol only waited a few minutes, which gave them just enough time to put their surgical gloves on and hide.

At approximately 11:30 p.m., Barbara was heard driving up to the garage by Marie Anne, who was in the bathroom, curling her hair. As Barbara got out of the car, she was surprised by Finch from behind. Through the open window in the bathroom, Marie Anne heard the sounds of a quarrel and then Barbara shouting her name for help. Bernie's anger was immediate and overwhelming. He cracked her skull with the butt of his gun, not once but twice. Astonishingly, she only lost consciousness temporarily. Bernie was at his wit's end and the apex of his anger.

How could she still be conscious?!

He'd never seen nor been taught a medical case where this happened.

Was there some divine force at work keeping her alive?

Was Bernie being given a last chance to stop the increasing violence?

If so, he didn't heed the warning. Carole and Bernie's meticulously planned murder now turned into a free-for-all with Barbara fighting back and Bernie unable to neutralize her so she could be sedated. Marie Anne ran out of the house in her bathrobe, further complicating matters by entering the garage. As she flipped on the light, she heard a woman's footsteps running away and the rustle of the bougainvillea bush.

Carole was gone and Marie Anne was now in the garage!

This was not how things were supposed to go down!

Although the car's engine was off, its radio and lights were on but no one in the garage was paying attention. Marie Anne saw Barbara lying on the garage floor with cuts on her head and Finch standing over her. She made a move towards Barbara, but Bernie, enraged, lunged at her and shoved her against the garage wall, flipping the lights off over her shoulder and banging her head into the wall at least twice, leaving a circular indentation in the plaster. Knocked senseless, Marie Anne collapsed and slid to the floor. Once she came to, she was in a different part of the garage and Finch ordered her to get into the back seat of the Chrysler. *Maybe Barbara's drive into the ravine was not a lost cause after all? She's just going to have a passenger.* Bernie shot his gun in the garage as a warning to Marie Anne. She got in the back seat of the car as Carole ran out of the bougainvillea bush and down the driveway to her car in the South Hills Country Club parking lot. Barbara rallied and Bernie half dragged/demanded she get into the front passenger seat. Sitting in the driver's seat, Bernie threatened to kill Barbara if she didn't give him the keys (but the radio was *on* and he then realized the keys were in the ignition). Barbara bolted and ran down the driveway towards her in-laws' home as Bernie gave chase, carrying the gun. Marie Anne got out of the car and ran back into the house. Patti opened the door to let her in and she heard a second gunshot, as did Carole, who was now a block away, nearing her car. Marie Anne called police. Fearing Finch would enter the home and shoot her, Marie Anne and Patti waited on the front lawn for police to arrive. Carole abandoned ship and—without Bernie—sped off in the DeSoto back to Las Vegas.

No matter how many hours she claimed she hid, she still had to pee. It was something never discussed at the trials nor was there ever any evidence she did so, willingly or uncontrollably from fear, hidden in the bush. Why didn't prosecutors bring this up with her on the witness stand? Probably because people didn't speak about bodily functions in court in the 1950s. But somewhere on her way back to Las Vegas, she stopped to relieve herself, if not mentally of the murder, at least physically of urine.

CHAPTER 13 – HOMECOMING

West Covina Police Officer Donald Rund was the first to arrive on scene and discover Barbara's body beneath a small tree in the corner of her in-laws' property. The Finches' Samoyed, Frosty, was barking nearby. Shot in the back near her right shoulder, the bullet coursed downward into Barbara's chest, severing the pulmonary artery leading to the left lung. The four-inch white satin cocktail pumps she had been wearing were found between the two homes, one twenty feet from her body in the driveway with its heel gone, the other within a yard of her body, indicating where she died. There were no signs of Barbara's purse, the bullet, its shell casing, nor the gun that killed her.

They would never be found.

But police lucked out, twice. First, West Covina Police Sergeant William Handrahan happened to live near where Carole and Jimmy Pappa once did in La Puente. He heard the police dispatch about Finch and knew not only that Carole was involved with Finch, but that she had recently moved to Las Vegas. Secondly, a Las Vegas sheriff's deputy heard about the hunt for Finch in town. He remembered having spoken recently to Carole about an expired license plate and he knew that she worked at the Sands Hotel. Sheriff's Detective Hiram Powell drove over to the Sands and found Carole working in the cocktail lounge, and without telling her why, asked for her address; she provided it. He called for backup to meet him at the Sands. When Detective Ray Gubser arrived, they headed for the apartment address to roust Finch from a sound sleep in Carole's bed.

Bernard Finch's love for his 1957 red Chrysler 300-C convertible was not as intense as his hate for his wife, Barbara. He was willing to sacrifice it and send Barbara's body in the car over an embankment next to their home, hopefully, masking her murder as an accidental death. (Photo credit Barrett-Jackson.com)

Los Angeles reporters got their first crack at Finch when he's escorted off the plane at Ontario International Airport the next day, Monday, July 20, by West Covina Police Sergeant William Ryan and Detective Ray Hopkinson. Wherein arresting officers in Las Vegas and momentary incarceration presented a certain gravitas for Finch, facing the phalanx of shouting reporters and motion picture and still cameras waving and flashing in his face must have been even more disconcerting. On another level, they massaged Finch's ego in a way seeing his name in the *Covina Argus-Citizen* when he was young never did: all this attention proved that Dr. Raymond Bernard Finch *was* King of the San Gabriel Valley. *Why would they be here otherwise?* Now Finch's desperate act to hold onto his kingdom was about to elevate him in to a tabloid stratosphere he would never return from.

The next day, July 21, saw a lot of action on the Finch properties. Carole arrived after having driven the previous day to stay with her parents in South Pasadena. She was fawned over by reporters and at the mercy of police as she lead them on her tour of the night Barbara died. Going unrecognized by police officers and reporters was the mink-trimmed collared suit Carole was wearing, taken from *La Maison de Barbara*, courtesy of Bernard Finch. Was Carole wearing this dressy suit Bernie "borrowed" from his wife's closet weeks ago on this very warm day in the sun an act to send a not-so-silent signal to Bernie?
I love you and we can get through this together.

In Las Vegas, Carole admitted to sheriff's deputies to being at Barbara's house on Saturday night, but not to any part in her death. She showed West Covina police where she hid in the bougainvillea bush while the battle between Finch and Barbara started. It conveniently gave her an alibi for not having participated in nor seeing what happened after she hid. Finch was also at the scene of the crime, escorted by Los Angeles County sheriff's deputies.

At the coroner's office downtown, Barbara's father, Walter Reynolds, sixty-three years old, identified his daughter's body, and was questioned by a reporter about Raymond's comment that his son was insane when he shot Barbara. "That's ridiculous," Walter told the reporter. "I think it's a hoax to get off. I hope he gets the gas chamber."

Since the morning after the murder, police scoured the Finches' properties, including the nearby South Hills Country Club golf course, for the murder weapon. They had no luck finding the gun, the bullet, or the shell casing. They were now using a metal detector, but still had no luck. Renowned criminal defense attorney Grant Cooper, who had been hired by Finch, arrived on scene; it's the first time the two men had met. Cooper, with Finch leading, was given a tour of the crime scene by police. When Cooper asked Detective Ryan where Barbara's body was discovered, Ryan pointed to the area and Finch nodded his head to Cooper, signifying the spot. Cooper then asked Ryan how many shots were fired.

"We don't know… we haven't found the gun yet."

Cooper and Finch had a private whispered conversation.

Did Finch tell Cooper where the gun was?

The police hoped the accommodating Finch would inadvertently reveal the gun's location. They followed as he led Cooper down the driveway from his home on a tour of the area. He stopped at the bottom on Lark Hill Drive, paused, and stared at the South Hills Country Club golf course across the street, playing his audience of police and reporters like a Stradivarius. He remembered out loud running through the orange grove across from the course to the other side that bordered Citrus Avenue. Anticipation built in his audience…

Was he referring to the stolen car or the gun?

Was Finch saying the gun was in the orange grove?

And then, as quickly as he had worked his audience into a silent, collective mental frenzy, he dropped them cold and shook his head.

"I honestly don't know."

Early that morning, Carole drove from her parents' house in South Pasadena to the Covina jail to see Bernie. She arrived early and brought him a suit to wear to court, but was told by an officer on duty that she would have to wait. After the scavenger hunt was over, Bernie was brought back to the jail to change into the suit Carole delivered. He was escorted to a patrol car to transport him to Citrus Court in West Covina for arraignment. Carole was given a few minutes to speak to him in the car before he left. She did so and emerged, smiling.

What did Finch say to her? Did he reassure Carole that he would not name her as his accomplice in any criminal proceeding?

Finch was arraigned in court by Judge Albert Miller, who set a hearing for the following Monday and remanded him to county jail, despite Cooper's plea for bail. Miller would also be preside over the hearing.

CHAPTER 14 – A LIFE INTERRUPTED

Friday, July 24, 1959

Oakdale Memorial Park, Glendora, California

Graveside

It was eighty-eight degrees in the warm, dry smoggy air as mourners gathered to lay Barbara Jean Finch to rest. Bernie's doubles tennis partner (and planned alibi for the day Jack Cody was to murder her) and assistant pastor of the First Presbyterian Church of San Diego, Dr. Alan Cheesebro conducted the graveside service. Among mourners in attendance were dancer/actress Vera-Ellen; au pair Marie Anne Lidholm; Barbara's brother, Jack Reynolds and her father, Walter Reynolds; her in-laws, Raymond and Marian Eva Finch, and Dr. Franklin Gordon and his wife, Marian Louise Finch Gordon; and in-laws, William and Jane Finch Wagner. Notably absent was Dr. Bernard Finch, whose petition to be released from the Covina jail to attend was denied by Judge Lewis Drucker, stating "it would be improper under the circumstances."

Earlier, conducting services at the Means Funeral Home in West Covina, Dr. Cheesebro spoke of Barbara as "the essence of charm. Cheerfulness radiated from her face. To be in her presence was to feel joy and delight." Now only the Finches buried nearby could feel her charm. They began to sing softly for those living who no longer could feel her presence nor hear them.

Down in the valley the valley so low
Hang your head over hear the wind blow
Hear the wind blow dear hear the wind blow
Hang your head over hear the wind blow

Roses love sunshine violets love dew
Angels in heaven know I love you
Know I love you dear know I love you
Angels in heaven know I love you

If you don't love me love whom you please
Throw your arms 'round me give my heart ease
Give my heart ease love give my heart ease
Throw your arms round me give my heart ease

Build me a castle forty feet high
So I can see him as he rides by
As he rides by love as he rides by
So I can see him as he rides by

Write me a letter send it by mail
Send it in care of Birmingham jail
Birmingham jail love Birmingham jail
Send it in care of Birmingham jail

America and Thomas Finch, among the Finches buried nearby, mourned, not only Barbara's death but the shame their descendant, Bernard, had brought to the family name.

From behind bars, Bernie sent his regrets.

PART II

CHAPTER 15 – *PERRY MASON* TIME

The Los Angeles Superior Courthouse in West Covina, known locally as the Citrus Court, and its jurist, Albert H. Miller, shared a milestone in 1959. The single-story, brickfronted courthouse opened that May, reflecting the past decade of exploding growth in the Eastern San Gabriel Valley. Judge Miller turned seventy-five the same month. A native Ohioan, Miller ran his courtroom as though it were in a small Midwestern town from the previous century. If one squinted their eyes in his courtroom they might have seen Miller smoking his pipe, feet propped up on a pickle barrel next to a potbelly stove, waiting for his checkers opponent to make the next move.

Miller had been practicing law for fifty years but had only been on the municipal bench for five. He had deep convictions about the foundations on which his country was built and went out of his way to make sure a person on the witness stand knew their rights. His courtroom had a certain folksy informality, but there was also a line no one wanted to cross to stay on his good side. Miller was known for kicking people out of his court who did not show deference to the law by being properly dressed. Men should be in business suits and women in dresses. No exceptions. There would be no ladies in his courtroom wearing those newfangled midcentury pedal pushers, capri pants, clam diggers, or whatever they may be called. Pants on women reminded Miller of ladies bloomers and he didn't cotton to women exposing their unmentionables in court.

That said, that Monday morning, July 27, 1959, Judge Miller was more worried about the high temperature. His ninety-nine seat courtroom was stifling hot and the new air conditioning system barely made an impact on the ninety degree heat outside that threatened to bake everyone inside. Miller had placed thermometers around the courtroom and as he moved around and warmly greeted both friend and foe of the court alike, he kept an eye on the rapidly rising temperature and notified his bailiff with each rising degree.

What's wrong with the air conditioning?

The bailiff notified Judge Miller that he had done everything in his power and a service man was on his way to work on the air conditioning. But that did not satisfy Miller. When the rising temperature reached *his* boiling point, Miller allowed the men in the courtroom to take off their coats. And it finally did—at eighty-two degrees. "The court will approve men taking off their coats," he surprised those present, who were near fainting due to wearing their required Sunday best in the suffocating indoor heat.

"Is that an order?" someone shouted to add some levity.

"Yes," Miller responded. Practically every man stood up and took off his coat. Miller let the ladies know he hadn't forgotten them. "Of course, you women haven't enough clothing to flag a handcar" (meaning they would not be allowed to remove anything). Unfortunate, since most of the people in the courtroom were women. Surprising for a man of the nineteenth century, Miller did not provide swooning beds in the lobby. Ladies who felt the vapors coming on would just have to rely on their corsets to keep them in a vertical position if they passed out from the heat.

Today would be the first of what would turn out to be a four-day hearing for Finch. Among the spectators were *Perry Mason* television series producer, Gail Patrick Jackson, and her husband, Cornwell Jackson, president of the Los Angeles

Judge Albert H. Miller, West Covina jurist for the Finch and Tregoff hearings. Miller will be later called as a witness at the murder trials. During his first appearance on February 1, 1960, Miller, a nonconformist to the end, is photographed lighting up his pipe with a large "no smoking" sign prominently hung behind him.

Tennis Club, where the Finches were members and where Barbara was last seen alive before she drove home. The courtroom was packed, surprising for a far-flung satellite of the Los Angeles Superior Court system. Over the weekend, news traveled quickly about the murder, and those present who had read about it or seen or heard it on television and radio and lived in the area either already knew the Finch name or were also patients at the West Covina Medical Clinic. Others just wanted to get a good look at Carole Tregoff, the "other woman" who had set events in motion. She did not disappoint.

Carole made her grand entrance in the mink-trimmed suit, heels, and wearing sunglasses. She could have been mistaken for either a movie star attending the premiere of her latest picture or one who, like Lana Turner recently, was about to play the real-life surprise witness at a murder trial. As Carole walked in, accompanied by her stepmother Gladys (who was also fashionably dressed), the two were barraged by flashes from photojournalists' cameras. Thus began a roadshow engagement of a real-life soap opera. It would have an eighteen-month run the public never tired of discussing, even decades after it ended.

Los Angeles County Coroner Gerald K. Ridge was the first person to take the witness stand. He testified to his findings of Barbara's body. West Covina Police Captain William Ryan was also questioned. Contents of the attaché case or the "murder kit" (as it was now branded by prosecutor Fred Whichello to the delight of reporters) were revealed to include .38-caliber bullets, clothesline, a butcher knife, two types of Seconal, needles, syringes, and a flashlight. When Finch was arrested in Las Vegas, Captain Ryan and his partner, Detective Ray Hopkinson, were given a set of keys found by Las Vegas sheriffs in Finch's wallet. One of the keys opened the attaché case. While awaiting the hearing over the weekend, Finch had broken down in jail and sobbed over his wife's death, claiming he had tried for a reconciliation for several months. "Everything in the bag is legitimate. I'm a doctor." The murder kit was popular with the press and widely photographed as though it were a Coney Island sideshow exhibit, with many involved in the case, including Finch, his attorney Cooper, and prosecutor Whichello, having their picture taken next to it or holding items found inside.

When it was Carole's turn up to bat, she frustrated Whichello by calmly testifying. Her story supported Finch's (particularly regarding the contents of the kit and their intended use as patient medicinal treatments) and that Barbara pulled the gun on the two of them. She contradicted Marie Anne's version of events at the Finch home the night Barbara died. During her drive back to Las Vegas she told Whichello that she heard a 5:15 a.m. radio chime, which was to establish her claim that she stayed hidden in the bougainvillea for hours. However, Carole didn't mention, nor was she asked, where on the highway she heard the 5:15 a.m. chime. Was it just after leaving the Finch home or closer to her Las Vegas apartment? If closer to Las Vegas, it would mean that she hot-footed it off the Finch property just after Bernie fired the first shot in the garage and was a block away when she heard the second shot, as she earlier told a reporter. If she heard the chimes closer to the Finch home, she would have actually spent somewhere between three to five hours hiding in the bush, but I've already given my reason earlier for why I don't believe that occurred. She may have been mentally able to zone out, but I doubt that her kidneys nor bladder had the same power of concentration.

If Carole stayed in the bushes for hours, as she claimed, it could have been no longer than four, due to the time of Barbara's death being close to midnight, and leaving no later than 4 a.m., due to her claim she arrived at her apartment in Las Vegas at 9 a.m. The drive from West Covina to Las Vegas would have been close to, if not at least, five hours in 1959 over the then two-lane highway at a slower speed limit with at least one-stop for gas and restroom needs. Even considering there would have been less traffic very early in the morning, Carole would not want to bring attention to herself by speeding. Did the prosecution ever calculate and/or use this in the trial(s)? Hiding in the bush for four hours is much less than the five or six she and her attorneys claimed and could have been used to trip her up. The prosecution believed, based on how long her car was seen in the South Hills Country Club parking lot, she was only at the crime scene ninety minutes, not the four to six hours she claimed. If so, she would have reached her apartment about the same time Finch did, which would have been about 6:30 a.m., plenty of time to get their stories straight before she had to be at work at 10 a.m.

Dr. Finch did not testify but gave reporter Mary Blair an exclusive interview, calmly telling her that "the prosecutor…is not producing anything damaging but he is presenting facts fairly. The witnesses in their testimony will tell a vindication for me."

Finch had been held in jail for nine days since his arrest in Las Vegas. Referring to his down time, he added, "This is the first rest or vacation I've had in eight or nine years." Finch said he received many letters and telegrams of support from the medical community, including his alma mater. "It makes me feel that my forty years of being a solid citizen in the community is being recognized. I'd say that I know everyone in the courtroom—most of them are my patients." Finch explained away his father's comment to the press that he was crazed and should have been put away with "he's old and has diabetes."

When it was Bernie's turn to be photographed with the murder kit, he could not keep his hands off the exhibits, including examining his wife's bloodied dress. Attorney Ned Nelsen, sitting in for Grant Cooper (who had a previous engagement out of town), looked over at Finch and saw him wearing the straw alpine hat with the exhibit tag dangling behind his head.

"Bernie, what are you doing?" Nelsen asked in horror of seeing his client unwittingly connect himself to the crime scene.

"Well, the fellas asked me to put it on," Bernie innocently replied, referring to the reporters who baited him for the photo op.

Finch models the evidenced-tagged alpine hat for reporters who cheered him on as his attorney looks up in horror at his client naïvely connects himself to the murder for a photo op.

CHAPTER 16 – THE CASE OF THE MINK-TRIMMED SUIT

On Wednesday, July 29, Carole Tregoff was questioned again on the witness stand by Deputy DA Whichello. The mild-mannered prosecutor started to dig deep about her relationship with Finch and finally asked if she had sexual relations with him.

"This is not a cheap relationship!" she cried out, breaking into deep sobs.

Judge Miller called for a recess, which she spent composing herself accompanied by her stepmother. In his chambers, Miller gave her some fatherly advice and told her if she just answered the question, they could move forward and she would be finished with her testimony, implying that she could go home. This in-chambers counsel would prove to be a keg of dynamite in the trials that followed. Miller would have to appear at all three to explain his action.

After composing herself and returning to the stand after the recess, Carole confirmed that she had intimate relations with Dr. Finch. "I assume the witness can be excused?" Judge Miller asked the prosecutor.

"Your Honor, she is going to be arrested as soon as she leaves the witness stand," Whichello informed the stunned courtroom, as reporters and photographers jumped to their feet, only to be ordered to sit back down by Miller.

Carole would be charged as a principal conspiring with Finch to murder Barbara. Carole looked first to Miller to save her (since he put her in this position) and, his failing to do that, then over to Finch. Finch jerked erect in his seat, stiffened, and grabbed hold of the counsel table; not only enraged over her arrest, but also likely because he had broken his promise to her in the patrol car to keep her out of the criminal proceeding. Carole was led from the stand by Ryan and Hopkinson outside. Reporters surrounded them and asked if she expected to be arrested.

"I certainly did not," she told them, possibly believing her arrest occurred because she told the court she had sex with Finch, *not* because they conspired to kill Barbara. And she may have had good reason to believe it. Announcing that you had non-marital sex with a married man in the 1950s wasn't that different from a woman in the 1600s who was found to have done the same, with one exception: Carole was unlikely to be burned at the stake.

Gladys, Carole's stepmother, shocked when she heard Whichello's announcement about Carole's arrest, was now in a manic state. She pleaded with anybody who would listen for help.

"What are they charging her with?!"

"What did they say she's done?!"

"Where are they taking her?!"

Apparently to jail.

Ryan and Hopkinson escorted Carole to the West Covina Police Department for booking. Deputy DA Whichello had smartly set up Carole to incriminate herself by getting her to admit being in love, wanting to marry, and having sexual relations with Finch. Her confirmation of a romantic relationship with Finch and knowledge of the contents in the murder kit established her probable role in a conspiracy to murder Barbara.

Whichello told reporters, "We are confident the two of them planned this thing together." Whichello added that the prosecution's theory was that the two were going to tie up Barbara, give her an overdose of Seconal, place her in the Chrysler, and send it over the cliff south of the home, but

*July 29, 1959 – West Covina Police Captain William Ryan
escorts Carole Tregoff after her arrest on the witness stand
at the Finch hearing out of the courthouse to be booked,
processed and held at the Covina Police Department (West
Covina Police did not have holding facilities at the time)*

Marie Anne's sudden appearance called for an adjustment with her addition to the airborne car.

"That young Swedish girl spoiled the whole thing," Judge Miller would later say.

At the police station, Carole's tears smudged the booking and fingerprint work. Ryan and Hopkinson questioned her for fifteen to twenty minutes, asking why she changed her story. She replied, "I had my reasons." Those "reasons" were intended to save Dr. Finch, but the end result was they backfired on her.

Ned Nelson arrived and told police Gladys had hired him to represent Carole. He advised her to not say anything *and* not to take the polygraph test she offered police. Finished being processed, she was allowed to sit on a bench, one wrist cuffed to the wall (since there were no holding cells), lean on a counter, and cry into the crook of her arm, her eyes shielded with a tissue from the world but not photographers who saw an opportunity for a memorable photo. She was then escorted back to the courthouse, where she was put in a holding cell to wait to be transported with Finch and other inmates to the county jail in downtown Los Angeles. Exhausted from her day-long ordeal, she passed out on a bench until it was time to be led away.

A short time later, Carole, Finch and other prisoners were escorted to a County Jail bus. Carole entered with another female prisoner, trailed by Finch who was chained to three other men but still managed to drag them along in an attempt to catch up to her. He attempted to sit behind Carole on the bus but a deputy prevented it, reseating him three rows away. As the bus drove off, Gladys, helpless and sitting on the courthouse steps, sobbed as she was interviewed by reporters. She reached, digging deep into her emotional pit, and cried out, recalling Carole's affirmation of sexual relations with Finch.

"Carole's not a tramp! She's *not!*"

Downtown, Carole wore a county-regulation denim dress and a pair of standard-issue saddle shoes that replaced her "gay, [red] high-heeled pumps." The red pumps would get a workout over the next few months. She was not allowed to have another pair of civilian shoes brought in from the outside due a rule that prevented shoes from being given to an inmate by a third party because they could potentially carry narcotics in their heels. Only Carole's manicured and lacquered nails escaped prison scrutiny and expulsion. The door slammed shut on her cell behind her. Carole was slapped with a reality she never counted on. When asked later by a reporter in jail if she would like to see Finch, she snapped back.

"*Who* said I wanted to see him?!"

On July 30, the fourth and last day of Finch's hearing, Judge Miller, in a twenty-eight minute summation that sounded more like a prosecutor's final argument, acknowledged that Dr. Finch and his father Raymond were friends of his. "I cannot consider my friendship with litigants in any court case. If that were so there would be no law at all." Since Finch abandoned his children, left his dead wife on the lawn, "and even left Miss Tregoff behind," Miller denied bail and moved Finch's case to Superior Court for arraignment in Pomona on August 17, 1959.

Bernie leapt to his feet and walked past his attorney Nelson, but stopped in his tracks when Miller called for the bailiff to escort him to the holding cell until he could be transported back to the county jail. Nelson still tried for bail, claiming a case for premeditation hadn't be made; it was denied by Miller. He asserted that *Barbara* was the one who pulled a gun on Finch and Carole. Deputy DA Whichello responded that the death penalty was very likely in the case and therefore bail should be denied. "The Court has the right to believe that somebody shot Barbara Finch from three feet away and the only person available to shoot her was Dr. Finch who ran down the hill chasing her down the driveway."

Finch took umbrage with the judge for denying him bail without hearing his side, and said, "My faith in the courts has been greatly shaken." He added, when he testified on his behalf, he could square discrepancies in Carole's and Marie Anne's testimonies, claiming what they *both* said was *true*, but since neither were present in the garage at the same time, they did not know everything.

Only he did.

Divide to conquer.

Marie Anne told reporters that the mink-trimmed suit Carole wore to the hearing on the first day was Mrs. Finch's. Barbara's friends who were present at the time noticed and commented on it. She stated that she and Barbara were cleaning out her closet and she noticed several of her dresses were missing. Marie Anne believed that Finch took them during the extended period Barbara was away from their home, staying with Marca Helfrich. When asked about the dress, Finch told reporters that his wife was a size 12-14 and Carole was a size 8-10, that their weights and heights were also much different, so the dress, although similar to one Barbara owned, couldn't be the one Carole was wearing. Carole also scoffed at Marie Anne's accusation.

Yet, what were the chances both women (one who had the means to buy it, the other who didn't) owned the same expensive, unusual suit?

Unless Dr. Finch bought one for *each* of them.

CHAPTER 17 – SUPERMAN'S ATTORNEY

A day or two later, Detectives Ryan and Hopkinson went to Las Vegas to search Carole's apartment again. They had little interest in who owned the minktrimmed suit. They were searching for other evidence to tie Finch to Barbara's death. They believed the market nearby Carole's apartment was where she and Finch bought the butcher knife and flashlight. Jo Bigelow, the clerk, identified Finch in photos. Ryan and Hopkinson bought similar items to compare to those in the murder kit back in West Covina.

Having spent a few days behind bars had a sobering effect on Carole. She told a reporter on August 2 that she no longer loved Finch. She was more interested in food at the moment. "I tell you, if I get out of this, I'm going home to my folks and eating all day. I'm always hungry. I'm hungry now." A short while later, she added, "I'll dye my hair and get lost."

James and Gladys Tregoff used their restaurant in downtown Los Angeles as collateral and hired famed Hollywood criminal defense attorney Jerry Geisler and his partner Robert Neeb to defend Carole. If Carole was to be seen as a high-profile celebrity, what better attorney than one who had a track record representing stars? Giesler had a long history defending notables such as Charlie Chaplin for violation of the Mann Act; Errol Flynn for statutory rape; Bugsy Siegel for his role in the murder of mobster Harry Greenburg; Robert Mitchum for illegal possession of "narcotics" (which marijuana was classified as at the time); Alexander Pantages (of the famous theater chain) for rape of a minor; and stripper Lili St. Cyr for—what else?—indecent exposure.

Giesler was currently representing Helen Besselo, *Superman* TV star George Reeves' mother, in an investigation into her son's death a month before Barbara's murder. Giesler had a record of acquittals and friends in high places. The Tregoffs were hoping he could work some of his Hollywood magic for their star Carole. They hired the firm just in time. Carole's hearing was scheduled for the next day, which Giesler's partner, Robert Neeb, asked the court for a week's delay to catch up, to which Whichello did not object.

Whichello gave Neeb a tour of the Finch residences and grounds with police and reporters tagging along on August 4. Whichello created one of the most iconic press photos of the Finch case when he laid down in the spot where Barbara died, in the same position as her body was found by police. He apparently had studied and memorized the police photo taken the night she was murdered. When District Attorney McKesson saw the photo, he likely thought it was in bad taste for one of his subordinates to playact a murder victim's death pose. If so, it may have been the first mark against Whichello even before the first trial began.

British author and screenwriter Eric Ambler, in his 1963 book, *The Ability to Kill*, described Whichello as having "the apologetic air of an amateur actor cast as Marc Antony in a charity performance of *Julius Caesar*, worried about the draping of his toga." It may have been that Whichello initially landed the Finch case because he worked out of a nearby court in Pomona and his calendar was open, and not because of any innate ability as prosecutor of high-profile murderers. Whichello would later be taken to task in the press for his polite, lackluster questioning of Finch in the first trial. By the time he decided to shift gears and

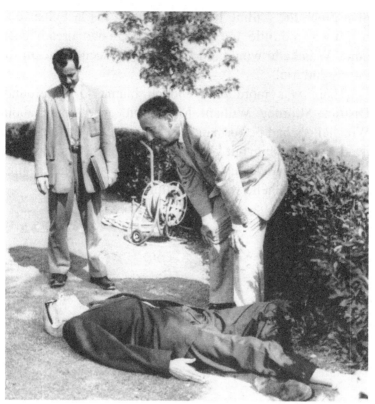

August 5, 1959 – Los Angeles County Deputy District Attorney Fred Whichello "lies down on the job" to show the position Barbara Finch's body was found by police for Carole Tregoff's defense attorney, Robert Neeb. Standing to the left is West Covina police captain, William Ryan.

give Finch the grilling he needed during his last chance at bat, it was too little, too late. The damage had already been done. Whichello would not be on the prosecution team for the second trial.

There was more than enough blame to go around. District Attorney William McKesson, who knew about Whichello's bad performance early on, could have stepped in and replaced him but failed to do so. Was there a reason he couldn't replace Whichello? Or was he just hoping against hope that Whichello would turn things around?

CHAPTER 18 – CAROLE, OH, CAROLE

On August 11, Carole's hearing was set to begin in Citrus Municipal Court, the scene of Dr. Finch's. But things were different this time. Word had not only spread beyond the San Gabriel Valley about the Finch murder, but built into a firestorm of cultural desire across Los Angeles, much like a Kardashian event today. A rowdy crowd of more than two hundred and fifty people, mostly women, teenagers, and a few scattered men, were fighting with marshals and police in a line *outside* the courthouse to make sure they got in. The building door finally opened and there was a stampede into the lobby. In a vicious adult game of musical chairs, people screamed and shoved each other against the closed door of a double set into the courtroom, unable to get through the one open door to fill one of only a hundred available seats. A woman was injured in the crush.

Once the seats were filled, sheriff's deputies tried to hold back others, but some still managed to burst through the door to stand in the back of the courtroom against the wall. Judge Martin allowed them to remain and instructed the bailiff to keep order.

"I wanted to see if Carole looked like her pictures in the paper; she's prettier," one pregnant young woman told a reporter. A college psychology student was asked why people turned up for these kind of events, but she refused, saying, "It would not be very complimentary," excluding herself. Other spectators appeared because they "live around the corner" or were there to pay a traffic citation and got caught up in the frenzy.

Carole's attorney Robert Neeb opened the proceeding by charging that Carole's rights were violated on the witness stand during the Finch hearing due to self-incrimination.

On August 13, Neeb got Los Angeles County Coroner Clifford Cromp to admit that the gun that killed Barbara could have been fired from as little as two feet, opening up the possibility that it could have been even closer and accidentally discharged in a struggle between Finch and his wife. Las Vegas Sheriff's Detective Hiram Powell testified that upon receiving the teletype from West Covina Police, he drove over to the Sands Hotel to speak with Carole in the cocktail lounge where she was working. She gave him her address and told Powell that Finch was there but that he had been with her all weekend. He and Detective Ray Gubser arrested Finch and booked him at the department. Carole called Powell later when she got home from work. Powell and Gubser arrived at her apartment and she agreed to a search. The three of them packed Finch's belongings for the detectives to take. She told them that she and Finch drove to West Covina the previous evening. His interest piqued, Powell asked Carole to an interview at the station and she agreed, driving back with the men and Finch's belongings.

Other witnesses this day included Detective Ryan and Marie Anne. When Marie Anne described Dr. Finch turning off the lights in the garage when she entered, the lights in the courtroom went out and then come back on momentarily.

Judge Martin, with a slight smile on his face asked "Is the defendant still here?"

Robert Neeb quipped, "Yes, Your Honor, the lights weren't out long enough."

Everyone laughed—except Carole.

The next day, August 14, was my eighth birthday party and while I contemplated George Reeves' leap off the roof of his Brentwood home while looking up at mine, prosecutor Fred Whichello questioned Carole again about her intimacies with Dr. Finch. If I had seen the *San Gabriel Valley Tribune* front page headline that day, would I have asked my mother what a "love nest" was? Would she tell me that's where birds lay their eggs?

Is that what Finch and Carole were doing in their apartment?

Whichello was called to the witness stand by Neeb to explain arresting Carole Tregoff earlier on the witness stand. "This is the chance he has been waiting for for years," Whichello told the judge.

"I'd like to go on record as saying that this is my first opportunity at cross-examining a deputy district attorney," Neeb retorted. Whichello claimed that his exam of Carole was not premeditated to trap her into incriminating herself, but once he realized her testimony conflicted with what she told police in Las Vegas, he decided to arrest her as an accomplice.

Did Carole give evidence in violation of her Constitutional rights?

It would be the key factor in Judge Martin's decision to either dismiss murder charges against her or move her to trial. The answer came soon enough. Four days later, on August 18, Carole was indicted for murder due to her conflicting accounts regarding the murder kit, seeing/ not seeing Barbara Finch run down the driveway, and her arraignment testimony. Judge Martin conceded that there was no precedent in California law for admitting testimony which violated a witness's Constitutional rights, but he managed to cobble other evidence together within the law he relied on to come to his decision. Carole was arraigned with Dr. Finch on August 31, 1959.

Before she was taken back to jail, Carole was handed a registered letter. It was from Finch's father Raymond, with a twenty dollar bill for her to purchase personal care items behind bars. Always ready to anticipate someone's needs and serve them during his optometry and jewelry business days, Raymond had not forgotten that there was a second defendant in his son's murder case who needed more primping behind bars than Bernie.

On August 31, Bernie pled not guilty to murder and his trial was set to begin November 24 in Pomona Superior Court. Carole's plea was continued until September 14. District Attorney William McKesson wanted to try both of them together in a theory of conspiracy to murder. Grant Cooper asked for a motion to suppress attorneys from talking about the case to the press, but Judge Whyte denied it, allowing them to leave it to "the good judgment of counsel." Two weeks later, he heard arguments as to whether Carole's testimony against herself should be admitted. Two days later, she was released from jail on a twenty-five thousand dollar bond, which her parents and friends raised. Carole grabbed her red satin pumps (sans narcotics, of course) on her way out and left with her parents for their South Pasadena home.

CHAPTER 19 – A
CONSPIRACY OF DUNCES

The next day, Carole played piano for a newspaper photo op at her parents' home as childhood friend and reluctant rat Don Williams stood on the steps of the Las Vegas Sheriff's Department. He told reporters that Carole asked him to put her in touch "with some tough guys who could take care of somebody." Protecting his childhood friend, he backpedaled on "take care of somebody" by saying he believed she meant to "get some dirt" on Barbara to prove she had an affair. After he heard that Barbara had been shot and killed, according to Don, conman Jack Cody contacted him (likely from Milwaukee) saying that Finch and Carole still owed him money, although he did not tell Don why.

Did Cody think Finch and Carole had hired someone else to do the job and that he would try to claim the murder since they weren't at the scene? Did the thought cross his mind that they *might have committed the act?*

The following day, September 18, DA McKesson told the press that he was seeking to arrest those same "tough guys," John Patrick "Jack" Cody and Richard Allan Keachie, as co-conspirators who had been given up to police by Don. Don was now recanting his earlier statement to reporters, stating police badgered him into saying it. Did he forget that sheriffs had recorded his interview?

It didn't matter; Keachie was already in custody in Las Vegas. He had been caught and arrested in a motel room, acting as a pimp for two sex workers. Before they were picked up by police, Don visited Keachie in the motel room and the women overheard them discussing hiring a third party to do away with Barbara. When they're arrested, the women ratted out Don and Keachie to police to gain their release. Keachie initially refused to cooperate with sheriffs, but eventually both he and Don, after reaching deals with the sheriff's department, agreed to cooperate with authorities and testify before a jury in Los Angeles.

Jack Cody was under detention, but more than fifteen hundred miles away in Minneapolis. He had been arrested in Milwaukee and returned to the city where he had previously escaped from the workhouse and, on the lam, traveled to Las Vegas.

Whichello and Captain Ryan traveled to Minneapolis to interview him. A photo of Carole had been found in Cody's wallet, confirming Don's earlier statement to sheriffs that he had given one to Keachie and Cody. Still, Cody denied that he was paid to kill Barbara Finch. He demanded a lawyer and refused to make a statement. Eventually, he decided to cooperate after a deal was offered.

He told Whichello and Ryan that Finch paid him $1,400 "to do away with somebody" in early July in Las Vegas, but he never made good on his promise and gambled the money away. He told Whichello that Carole gave him a $350 down payment to buy a gun and a plane ticket to Los Angeles to kill Barbara. He arrived in Los Angeles, stayed a few days, and returned to Las Vegas, asking for the rest of his money. "Okay, I've done my job, give me the rest of the money." Carole gave him the remaining $830.

To confirm the murder, Dr. Finch called his home but Barbara answered, very much alive. Finch now demanded that Cody go back to Los Angeles and do what he was paid to, and put him drunk on a plane. Cody sobered up during the flight and upon landing, got a friend to drive him back to Las Vegas, where he retrieved his personal belongings and left town, heading east. Cody told Whichello he never intended to kill Mrs. Finch. He signed his statement, which included agreeing to act as a prosecution witness in Los Angeles.

Back in Los Angeles, Carole's attorneys filed an appeal claiming her Constitutional right against self-incrimination was denied by Judge Miller in West Covina. They were also trying to separate her case from Finch's. DA McKesson was now thinking of rescinding her bail. A reporter called Carole late in the evening at her parents' home in South Pasadena, rousting her from sleep and asked for comment, but she declined. To prevent her from fleeing, investigators followed her every move, waiting in a car parked across the street from her parents. In the background of a press photo they can be seen sitting in a car as she pulls the mail out of her family's curbside box. Later, driving within the speed limit to a meeting with Robert Neeb, she looked in the rearview mirror and noticed she had lost her tail. At the next stoplight, she waited for the DA's investigators to catch up to prove, according to Neeb, that she had no intention of fleeing.

It was a far cry from the times she and Finch eluded Barbara's private investigators.

CHAPTER 20 – DAZED
AND CONFUSED

When Deputy DA Whichello returned to Los Angeles after interviewing Jack Cody, he told the press he may seek the death penalty and revocation of Carole's bail due to her role in Barbara's murder. The following day, DA McKesson expressed his concern to Judge Whyte that Carole may be a flight risk. Whyte ordered Carole to show cause in court as to why her bail should not be revoked or post a one hundred thousand dollar bond. He later decided not to revoke her bail, saying she would have already fled, but didn't, when she heard from the reporter during his late night phone call about the potential revocation. But just when she might have had cause to celebrate her continued freedom that day, she had been served a subpoena for an appearance in front of a grand jury.

During the hearing, Robert Neeb attacked the conspirators' evidential credibility—two of them were in jail for felony charges.

Whichello replied, "The district attorney is not the casting director; the defendant is."

Judge Whyte ruled against Whichello, stating that a thorough investigation before Carole's hearing could have produced the evidence he had come back with from Minneapolis. It was also known that one of the new witnesses, Don Williams, was living in the same house as the defendant at the time of Barbara's murder. Why hadn't Whichello interviewed him early on?

On October 5, escorted by a sheriff's deputy, Jack Cody flew into Los Angeles to testify in front of a grand jury. When he departed the plane, he was asked by reporters about his take on Carole. "She seems to be a very nice person but I guess even nice people sometimes have bad thoughts."

Judge Lewis Drucker set aside an order that required Carole to testify at the grand jury. One of her attorneys, Donald Bringgold, had won a dismissal of the subpoena which would have required her to testify on the basis that whatever she said on the stand could be used against her. Due to the decision, Whichello would also not require Finch to testify. But all other prosecution witnesses did so the following day.

Cody, in his distinctive con artist style, told skeptical jurors his story, which included payments made to him by Carole and Finch for which he did not fulfill the agreement. Next on the stand, Don Williams supported Cody's testimony. Among statements in Cody's favor were specifics about the Finch home in his testimony that he would have only known by being told by Finch or Carole, such as the garage door remote was broken and the family dog, Frosty, was too old to hurt anyone. Cody also told the grand jury that Carole initially sketched the layout of the Finch home and the neighborhood on a cocktail napkin one evening, replacing it with a more elaborate drawing the next day, which included the Hollywood apartment where Barbara Finch was staying with friends.

Don testified that he introduced Carole initially to Richard Keachie, who introduced her and Finch to Cody. Cody was a selfprofessed ladies' man, who, if he couldn't get extra-marital goods on Mrs. Finch, said he would sexually compromise her himself. Murder never mentioned, though police claimed otherwise. Asked later if the grand jury believed him, Williams replied, "If I were that good of a judge of character, I wouldn't be involved in this."

On October 7, 1959, the grand jury (based primarily on Don Williams' testimony supporting Jack Cody's) indicted Dr. Bernard Finch and Carole Tregoff for murder. Trying to absolve himself of his role in determining Carole's fate, Don told reporters, "Carole never mentioned anything about murder or violence. I never had any idea there was a job to be done."

The following day, Judge Drucker arraigned both Finch and Carole for murder in Superior Court. Her bail was revoked and she was returned to jail, pending trial.

CHAPTER 21 – HALL
OF JUSTICE

On October 16, Marie Anne sued Dr. Finch for one hundred thousand dollars for attacking and physically harming her during the murder of his wife by knocking her head into the garage wall. On November 4, even though her attorneys attempted to quash her involvement in the Finch case due to a constitutional rights violation, Judge John Barnes ordered Carole to stand trial with Dr. Finch starting December 1 in Pomona Superior Court. Two days later, Finch's attorney, Grant Cooper, requested a change of venue to downtown Los Angeles to keep his client (and, due to Barnes' order, Carole) from making a daily roundtrip from the downtown jail to Pomona that would deny conference time with the attorneys and "warm lunches."

On October 7, it's revealed through Lyle Daugherty filing a suit on behalf of his daughter Patti the previous July 25 (a week after Barbara's death) that Dr. Finch had assigned all his personal properties—including his hilltop home in West Covina, his cars, boat, and interests in West Covina Medical Clinic, Hospital and Labs, and other properties—to Grant Cooper to pay for his legal fees, which started with a twenty-five thousand dollar retainer, and based on a three hundred and fifty dollar per-day trial rate (approximately $222,000 and $3,100, respectively, in 2020). What Finch once feared he would lose to Barbara in a divorce, the primary reason he murdered her, was now handed over to Grant Cooper to save Finch's neck. When factoring in the three trials and his time behind bars that followed, even if Barbara got everything, it would have been less expensive to his well-being if he had just divorced her. He also wouldn't be potentially facing the gas chamber for her death.

The Hall of Justice (HOJ) is located downtown in the city block intersected by Spring, Broadway, and Temple Streets, where steps lead up from Temple to the main entrance. The HOJ first opened in 1925 and served as the home for the Los Angeles County court, coroner, sheriff's office, county jail, and district attorney's offices. The building is familiar to many film and television viewers including fans of *Dragnet* and *Perry Mason*. Deceased notables who were autopsied in its coroner's department include Marilyn Monroe and Robert Kennedy. By the time the 1994 Northridge Earthquake closed the historic building due to extensive damage, the coroner had already moved. The HOJ was retrofitted and re-opened in 2015. The Finch-Tregoff trial began there on December 8, 1959.

Department 105 on the eighth floor of the HOJ had few seats in its courtroom, but many were taken by the fifty reporters and photographers with spectators filling the remaining fifty. Those not able to get in waited in a long line, which wound down the hall outside the courtroom, around the corner, and down another hall. Finch and Cooper were left without counsel seats due to the three that were provided were already occupied by Carole, Donald Bringgold, and her new lead attorney Rexford Eagan (Robert Neeb had left the case due to picking up cases an ailing Jerry Giesler was handling). Finch's pastor, Reverend Henry Kent of the Presbyterian Church of West Covina, asked to speak to him before the proceeding and was granted permission.

It's interesting to note this documented reference to a religious faith for Finch, other than the Church of the Brethren. When did Finch leave one denomination for another? Did Barbara's death compel the Brethren to ask Finch to leave? Or had it done so years before when Finch's drinking, drunken driving and womanizing couldn't be overlooked like it had been by so many others, including the police, the hospitals and medical clinics, the communities he lived in, even his own family and friends?

Once Finch and Cooper were finally provided seats, Cooper immediately tried to get the trial moved out of the county. Cooper claimed Finch couldn't get a fair trial with all the attendant publicity, including local Los Angeles-area newspaper articles (which were presented) and a filmed TV interview (which was screened) with Whichello by KCOP's newscaster Baxter Ward, who was also called as a witness.

Whichello believed Cooper's request to move the trial was a ruse to split it into two, but did concede it would be difficult to get twelve jurors who had not already been swayed to form a pre-existing opinion due to all the attendant local hoopla. Carole's lawyers, Eagan and Bringgold, also objected to Cooper's motion to move the trial because they claimed she did not have the funds to pay her counsel for a trial outside the county and wanted to be judged by a group of her local peers. They also wanted her trial separated from Finch's. Judge Walter Evans, who had been brought in from Mono County due to charges of local judges being biased, stated he would consider Eagan's motion once Cooper's motion for a change of venue was considered after proceeding through jury selection.

In addition to Whichello and local newspapers, Cooper also had District Attorney McKesson on his hit list. He wanted the jury to see a television interview with McKesson that he felt was prejudicial to Finch's case. Because the interview was recorded on the relatively new videotape format and few machines to play it existed at the time, courtroom participants made a field trip to television station KTLA to view it.

The next day, Cooper called Whichello to the stand and grilled him about statements he made to the press about the case. Frustrated he could not get information on record, Cooper called himself as a witness—then asked and answered questions of himself.

Cooper also produced a female pollster as a witness, to which second prosecutor Clifford Crail objected because the woman had never tested public opinion on the guilt or innocence of someone accused of murder. Nonetheless, she was allowed to provide testimony. It's interesting to note that, among her poll tallies, more men than women thought Carole Tregoff was innocent. Now all Carole needed was an all-male jury she could play to, but unfortunately she ended up with one evenly divided between male and female jurors. Among the male jurors are an AfricanAmerican and a Latino, a rarity for high-profile murderers who are white in 1959.

The rope in the "murder kit" allegedly used for Finch's boat is discussed with West Covina Judge Albert Miller, who has been called as a witness, commenting that the only boat the rope could be used on is one in a bathtub, suggesting that it wasn't strong enough to moor an adult-sized speedboat. Cooper handed a strand to Whichello and asked, "Have you ever used that kind of rope to sail a boat in a bathtub?" Whichello smiled and admitted he had not.

The next day's *Los Angeles Herald-Express* began a series of high-profile guest writers commenting on the trial. Author and screenwriter of *Red River* and *Winchester 73*, Borden Chase's column appeared first. He compared the Finch-Tregoff case to a three-act story whose third act had yet to be written. He claimed the story wasn't good to begin with because it's true and true stories are usually unbelievable. He also stated that Carole was miscast and couldn't have possibly done what the prosecution was claiming. Finch was flawless because he played his role "with ease and perfection." Finch also got points for not smiling, possibly Borden's allusion to the many westerns he had written where anyone who cracked one was asking for trouble. Maybe Borden was *confused* about film production.

After all, he called for "camera—lights—action!" in his column. Anyone familiar with the correct order of words in the phrase knows that film can't be exposed without light.

CHAPTER 22 – THE CIRCUS ROOM

The trial was creating such attention with the courtroom and hallways of the Hall of Justice so packed that a decision had been made to move the proceedings to a larger venue the next day. Trial participants met nearby in Department 12 in the new county courthouse in a chamber known as the Hippodrome, or Circus Room, for its immense size, with space for 263 spectators. Screenwriters and *Herald-Express* guest reporters, Joe Stone and Paul King, described the Circus Room in their article.

> Paneled in light colored oak sections, illuminated by a huge square, sectional skylight and indirect lighting, the new courtroom features a concave shaped floor to ceiling marble backdrop for the bench, and a long mahogany table for defendants, their counsel and attorneys for the prosecution. There is nothing austere or foreboding about the décor of this courtroom and it is difficult to believe that two people are on trial for their lives here— until Carole Tregoff and Dr. Finch arrive.

Over the course of three trials, reporters tried to intuit what Finch and Carole were thinking at any given moment by describing their facial expressions and body language. The concurrent reports only ended up contradicting each other as reporters failed to enter the guarded minds of the defendants.

Lead prosecutor Whichello and DA McKesson were called as witnesses to explain the timing of their statements to the press about information Whichello had obtained in Minneapolis as it was prejudicial to the defendants getting a fair trial in Los Angeles County. When asked by Cooper, Whichello denied that he coined the phrase "the do-it-yourself murder kit" for the attaché case and its contents found on Finch's front lawn. "I have to give credit to Captain William Ryan of the West Covina Police Department for originating that term" he told Cooper and the court. He did admit that the phrase was catchy and had received a lot of attention by the media, but denied using it at Finch's preliminary hearing to get attention.

Jury selection began with Cooper acting on the belief that impartial jurors could not be found. The first potential juror was dismissed when he stated that he was the former superintendent of the Iowa State Penitentiary shoe factory. After Cooper questioned potential jurors, they were then questioned by Carole's team, and then by prosecutors Clifford Crail and Fred Whichello.

The next day, Finch's civil attorney, Glenn Martineau, appeared with a document to sell and transfer his membership in the South Hills Country Club. "But this will mean I'll lose my tennis court privileges," Finch protested, seemingly oblivious to the threat that prison bars—let alone the gas chamber—should take precedence over his concern with tennis. Guest reporter and screenwriter Michael Fessier noted Finch's mental state during this period at the trial: "If his face portrays any emotion, it is not concern. Rather, his is the detached clinical demeanor of a surgeon witnessing an operation until the result of which depends on someone's life other than his own." To say Finch wasn't connected to the reality of what was going on around him was an understatement. Did Finch think his white male privilege extended from drunk driving passes to beating a murder rap?

"McKesson Called as Witness in Finch Case" appeared in the *Herald-Express* this day above a non-related photo with the caption, "Guns Found in Garbage Can." If the West Covina Police or the DA's office saw the page, it should have engaged their thought processes since the revolver that killed Barbara still hadn't been found. Had *anyone* in law enforcement stretched their powers of deduction momentarily, connected the two, and considered the possibility Finch may have disposed of the gun that killed Barbara in a similar fashion? If someone did, there's no written account, nor was the gun ever found—in a trashcan or otherwise.

The next day, jury selection continued. Cooper asked one potential juror if he had seen the television program *Mr. District Attorney* and whether the fact that the fictional prosecutor was always the hero would influence him. The juror, a man, replied no. In response to Cooper's question, Whichello cracked, "Ask him about *Perry Mason*." Cooper apparently was on edge during jury selection. At one point, he stopped the proceedings and told Judge Evans he heard a movie camera grinding away. Since photographs and television newsreel film could only be shot during recesses, a search was made for the errant photographer. It turned out to be a spectator who was getting a drink from a noisy fountain in the courtroom.

The Conciliation Court, where Finch and Barbara were once scheduled to appear, was directly across from the courtroom where Finch and Carole were now being tried. It was unlikely Finch noted the irony; he was too busy trying to get Carole's attention at the counsel table by cupping his hands and whisper-cooing, "Carole... Carole.... Carole." Possibly cognizant of the irony, she ignored him.

As jury selection neared its end, it was not without contention. While questioning a prospective juror, Rex Eagan told them there was no assertion by the prosecution that Carole fired the gun that killed Mrs. Finch. Whichello jumped to his feet. "I have not objected before because I assumed that the statement would be followed by a question." Eagan responded, "I am somewhat taken by surprise. Is it the contention of the prosecution that my client fired the fatal shot?"

Second prosecutor Crail entered the fray. "If counsel would disclose his defense, I would be glad to tell you."

"Our defense sits right here at the counsel table," Eagan responded.

He did not elaborate.

On Christmas Eve, Carole's petition to have a hearing in front of the Supreme Court was denied by Justice William O. Douglas. Eagan wanted the justices to consider his claim that there was no evidence of Carole's involvement in a conspiracy taking place in California to murder Barbara. Although Whichello had no physical evidence of Carole and Finch conspiring together in the state, he well knew that as early as two months before Barbara was killed, it was likely the two had already planned for the Chrysler to go over the embankment of the Finch home before they decided to hire Jack Cody. They may have well been planning her death much earlier than May, but since Barbara had stopped Investigator Lewis from continuing his surreptitious audio recordings, there were no tapes that might have recorded them discussing her murder.

On Christmas day, I received a beautiful, bright candy-apple red and chrome fender Schwinn 3speed bike, possibly, in part, as hush money because I cried when my mother told me a month earlier that she was going to have another baby. "You just had one!" I replied, as though it was something my mother had complete control over, noting my second sister's recent delivery by Finch's brother-in-law and medical center partner Dr. Gordon just thirteen months earlier.

Four days later, jury selection concluded in our former family doctor's murder case. I fell off my new bike and cut my inner lower lip on the left side. I was taken to West Covina Medical Clinic for stitching. My lip hurt too much in the lobby before the procedure and was too numb after on the way out, preventing me from possibly acting up and asking the receptionist why Dr. Finch didn't perform the procedure.

CHAPTER 23 – ANOTHER OP'NIN' ANOTHER SHOW

A cold snap finally broke over Los Angeles by a Santa Ana wind that roared through the basin, blowing over trees, power lines, and patio roofs as the Finch-Tregoff trial got underway on January 4. Finch's plea for a trial in another county and Carole's for a separate trial were denied the previous week by Judge Evans after jury selection was finalized. Evans qualified his two decisions based on his sampling the attitudes of prospective jurors. Those selected impressed him as being "alert, down to earth, and honest." Jurors' names, ages and addresses were published in the *Herald-Express*. Such specific juror identifying information would never be published today.

The wire recordings Barbara's investigator had made at the defendants' love nest were introduced by Whichello to establish a long romantic relationship between them. There are no published accounts of what was contained on the tapes nor what ultimately happened to them. In all likelihood, there must have been at least some damning conversations between Finch and Carole about Barbara that could have been used to their states of mind leading to the murder. The thought that these tapes may still exist, and could be found, is tantalizing. If they were not destroyed in a purge of the case's physical evidence after conviction, they would be the Holy Grail for all contemporary Finch-Tregoff fans to get their hands on. Could they still be sitting in an evidence box in the same DA's offsite facility where the trial transcripts are housed in the San Fernando Valley? Is it possible the tapes still exist?

Perry Mason producer Gail Patrick Jackson and her husband, Cornwell, last seen at the opening of the Finch hearing in West Covina the previous July, also attended opening statements this day. When Finch spotted Cornwell sitting behind him he foot-rolled his chair over to catch up on tennis. But someone even more famous and the most recognized celebrity to attend the trial was just about to arrive: *What's My Line?* panelist and newspaper columnist/reporter Dorothy Kilgallen (known to those close to her as Dolly Mae).

Kilgallen was not traditionally beautiful, a fact she was well aware of and occasionally reminded about when certain celebrities and columnists publicly denigrated her looks, particularly her chin, or lack thereof, when they felt she had wronged them in one of her columns. She may have been famous and tough, but their vicious remarks still deeply wounded her in a way nothing else did. Even without being model beautiful, she knew how to create an air of glamour. She dressed like the Broadway/Hollywood princess she was due to her famous newspaper reporter father, Jim Kilgallen, who first trail blazed a career she would follow.

She also knew how to make an entrance like Queen Elizabeth, whose coronation she covered in London in 1953. Kilgallen was reporting on the Finch-Tregoff trial for the Hearst newspaper syndicate (her first murder trial since Dr. Sam Sheppard's, also for his wife's death five years earlier). She made her grand entrance, arriving in the courtroom trailed on either side by a copy boy, one with her typewriter and the other her instruments of the trade. She dropped her boys off in the press section and was greeted like a queen by Judge Evans, who pinned an orchid on her lapel.

Kilgallen interviewed Finch and Carole several times over the course of the trial, more than any other reporter. For support this first day of the trial, Kilgallen brought her friends, actor Clifton Webb, ice skater Sonja Henie, and society maven, Cobina Wright (*"Now darling, are you sure it's going to be interesting today?"*). If they were less classy, there would have been popcorn. And if that weren't enough, Dorothy—who was smitten with good-looking young men like popular blues torch singer Johnnie Ray— became friendly during the trial with two court bailiffs, John Martin and Joe Sweet. She frequently mentioned them in her column, stating she was going to refer each to a movie studio (*but not the same one*), and allegedly went as far as arranging a screen test for one.

Fred Whichello spent over three and half hours laying out his case, using maps and diagrams of the Finch home in a dry tone similar to a college professor outlining his course over a semester. Whichello's manner may not have kept the courtroom awake, but the content—no professor could be describing which included conspiracy to murder a socialite and execution of the plan—did. In a surprise statement, he accused Finch of striking Barbara a third time on the head above the left eye, saying it wasn't initially noticed by the coroner because it didn't draw any blood. Barbara was already dead when Finch likely clubbed her again with the gun, laying out for the jury the scale of violence Finch was capable of.

Whichello's primary focus during his prosecution summary is based on the tape recordings made at Finch's and Carole's first apartment. He told the jury that the two had a romantic relationship "for years" that began in 1957, long before they and their defense attorneys would admit, setting the stage for the murder. As Whichello detailed Carole's sexual adventures with Finch over the years, the color ran from her face and she closed her eyes in embarrassment of the relationship being splayed open during the prosecutor's operation for all to see. Her demeanor suddenly changed and she bristled when Whichello claimed Finch paid the rent on their apartment. She looked to her attorney Rex Eagan for reassurance and he winked at her.

Grant Cooper requested the jury visit the Finch home the next day to familiarize itself with locations on the property that would be discussed during the trial. Whichello had no objection and Judge Evans agreed, asking the bailiffs to make preparations for a field trip to the top of Lark Hill Drive at 1:15 p.m. the next day. Evans adjourned court at 4:25 p.m. Carole and Finch had two different reactions to Whichello's having laid out his damning prosecution. Finch chatted and laughed with the Jacksons, Kilgallen, Webb, Henie, and Wright. Carole, without looking back at Finch or those surrounding him, made a hasty retreat for the door, out into the gusty Santa Ana wind which she likely prayed would pick her up and whisk her away from the headache she now had and the nightmare she knew was to come.

*January 5, 1960 – Dr. Bernard Finch climbs the
seven dirt steps up from his father's lawn where
Barbara fell and died to his home's driveway
during the first jury's visit to the properties.*

CHAPTER 24 – THE HOUSE ON THE HILL, PART I

Following lunch the next day, Judge Evans, Finch, Carole, Cooper, Whichello, Eagan, Bringgold, the jury (twelve members plus four alternates), and legal staff exited cars on the semiprivate road leading up to the faded chartreuse and white-roofed Finch home in West Covina.

The family room (with direct access to the patio surrounding the swimming pool) befitted Finch's penchant for booze by being equipped with a bar with bamboo stools and a built-in booth with coral-colored imitation leather, which rested on a green linoleum floor. A long room, its ceiling was coral pink like the bar's booth, reminiscent of the South Seas watering holes Finch favored, like the Luau in Beverly Hills, where he and Carole once got their buzz on drinking scorpions.

The living room had angular modern furniture (like the best midcentury-built homes) on top of a light pepper gray carpet. This room also had an expansive window with a view that took in towering Mt. Baldy beyond in the San Gabriel Mountains, which was covered in snow during California winters, a view I also saw from my bedroom window in nearby Charter Oak.

The grounds to Finch's home had not been kept up since his arrest five and half months earlier. The lawn was dead, the bushes overgrown, and the pool had been emptied but trash still floated in the remaining stagnant water near the bottom that refused to drain. In a highly-populated suburban area, the house appeared odd, as though it was lifted from a modern-day ghost town and dropped on the hill. The scene was only missing tumbleweeds blowing by and a stranger riding into town on a horse who stopped, surveyed the scene, and hitched his steed to a post to see what all the brouhaha was about. And there was brouhaha with a capital B.

Large crowds had gathered on the grounds and spilled over downhill below to Lark Hill Drive. The large number of people was in sharp contrast to the abandoned state of the home. A hundred cars lined the public portion of the road that fronted the South Hills Country Club, leading to the Finch home's private driveway. Spectators stood next to their cars parked just off the pavement, some using binoculars trained up the hill on the courtroom party which had been cordoned off by West Covina police to preserve some sense of decorum. Finch's sisters were already at their parents' home and came out to greet him. They shared a private laugh, ignoring and being ignored, by Carole.

For Carole, seeing the home again five and half months after Barbara's murder brought that fateful night into razor-sharp focus, one she did not easily handle. Dr. Finch made his way over to his mother on her front lawn and, with tears in his eyes, leaned over to kiss the ailing woman in her wheelchair.

Judge Evans convened court on the driveway of the Finch home. As in the courtroom, Evans was the only one who could speak; no others present were allowed to do so, even with each other. When Evans pushed the button on a remote (which apparently had been fixed or replaced), the garage door opened, and Carole cried out as though escaping ghosts might grab and transport her back to the moment Barbara arrived home. The jury silently examined the garage and paid little attention to the half-empty paint cans, old magazines, and an outgrown child's tricycle; debris that a family leaves behind when it normally vacates a home. Still, there was one thing that was left behind that jurors made sure they didn't miss: the hole in the wall made by Marie Anne's head. After viewing the reporter's earlier enlarged hole, did jurors silently marvel at the durability of Marie Anne's skull?

The party exited to the patio and swimming pool behind the garage where many media photos were taken of courtroom participants milling around the empty pool. Dr. Finch stood at the edge with his hands clasped behind his back and pensively gazed into the shotcrete-filled hole. What shape was his ego in?

Was he trying to read his future in the tea-leaf trash's putrid water?

Or thinking of diving into the empty pool to end his life?

The group headed back to the garage for one last look. Judge Evans pointed out the light and garage door switches and, just in case jurors missed it the first time, the hole in the wall made by Marie Anne's head. They exited to the front lawn and viewed the bougainvillea bush thirty feet away, where Carole claimed she hid for hours.

Carole and Finch stood some distance away from the jury, looked in the opposite direction, north to the San Gabriel Mountains on the horizon, and then down to the South Hills Country Club below. Were they recalling a time not so long ago when they fantasized about their life together here above Lark Hill Drive? If only Barbara had played her role the way they directed in their minds, they wouldn't be in the mess they were now in. Or at least gotten away with it if Marie Anne hadn't crashed their party.

Carole cried at what once appeared to be within her grasp. Finch was bored. Today was a far different scene from years past when he and Barbara stood in the same spot at night and viewed the valley below before walking down to the courts for tennis or drinks in the clubhouse, where Barbara "sparkled with personality" and Bernie, although "laughing at a joke seemed a bit reserved and withdrawn," recalled South Hills Country Club members.

The courtroom party moved down the driveway to Finch's parents' yard. A bamboo rake stood in for Barbara's body on the elder Finches' property, but Bernie never looked at it. Instead, he kicked at two protruding pipes in the lawn away from the jury. Was Finch trying to say something about the pipes in regard to his wife's death, a reporter speculated. *Did Barbara receive her post-mortem head wound by falling on one of them?* Or is Finch trying to blame *them* for her death? Several people bumped into a hedge. "Watch out for these bushes. There's dust on them," Finch announced as he brushed it off Donald Bringgold's pants. Finch was allowed a brief visit with his disabled mother inside her kitchen. A short while later, Bernie exited the home, sobbing, as a reporter asked for comment. The other reporters, in tune with his sorrow, moved out of the way, allowing him to pass through their phalanx to head back downtown.

Marie Anne Lidholm, nineteen-year old Finch au pair, appears as a prosecution witness at the first trial on January 26, 1960.

CHAPTER 25 – MARIE ANNE

Very early in the morning on August 6, 1992, author James Jones called Marie Anne Lidholm. It had been thirty-three years since the murder, but as with all victims of crimes, the passage of time had not made a dent in the horror of that night for her. She had remained in California for about ten years after the three trials, marrying her American boyfriend and moving back to Sweden after their divorce. She married and divorced again, but not before giving birth to a daughter who was now the age she was during Barbara's murder.

Like Barbara, Marie Anne had a difficult childhood with her parents divorcing when she was fourteen and her mother financially struggling to provide for the family. Marie Anne saw herself in her daughter's reflection and it reminded her of the time during Barbara's murder. It was something she very rarely discussed with anyone, or on the rare occasion she did, she did not provide specifics about "the trouble" she experienced during her early days in California.

In advance of Jones' call, Marie Anne had dug up the letter Barbara had written her in 1958. In it, she described the parameters of taking care of her children if Marie Anne decided to accept the Finch au pair position.

"We have two children, a boy who is five years old and a girl almost eleven," Barbara wrote. "My husband and I are frequently away from home and we especially want a reliable girl here to look after the children when we are not here."

Marie Anne reflected on the impact the Finches still had on her life in 1992:

You know, I have dreams about living back there in that house with Mrs. Finch. Dr. Finch is not in the picture for some reason. It's just the two of us. Barbara Jean and me, taking care of the little boy and Patti... Sometimes I still have nightmares about what happened. I wake up scared. Or I'll see something that reminds me of that night. I think that if I could go back and talk to everyone, to the children, to the grandparents next door... You know, I guess I thought that if I didn't talk about it, it would just go away. Somebody told me that 'time heals all.'

But I don't think it does.

The day after the jury's visit to the Finch home, Marie Anne recounted the night of the murder five months earlier on the witness stand. When asked whether she saw or heard anyone in the bougainvillea bush, she said no, in stark contrast to what she initially reported to police. She then was cross-examined by Grant Cooper. She used his head to recreate how Finch held hers when he banged it into the garage wall.

Cooper next questioned what she was now saying on the stand versus her report to police the night of Barbara's death.

"At that time I didn't know Mrs. Finch was dead... when I was telling you this story... Afterward you have time to think clearly... to tell the truth... and you have to go to court and everything."

Confusion and stress due to Cooper's cross caused her to break down and she lowered her head into her hands and began to sob. This would be the only time Marie Anne lost her composure during the three trials. It was also her first time on a witness stand during a trial and she learned from the experience and didn't repeat her mistake.

Cooper asked if she would like to take a break. She nodded and hastily made an exit from the witness stand and out of the courtroom into the lobby to recover.

Court adjourned for the day.

CHAPTER 26 – THE MURDER KIT, PART II

January 7, 1960, was Bernard Finch's forty-second birthday. To celebrate, and to humanize him for the public, Grant Cooper brought in a cake with a candle for a photo op during lunch in a court anteroom. Interest had been mounting throughout the trial and now all spectator seats were filled in the courtroom. Those who were not able to get in patiently waited in line in the lobby for empty seats.

Marie Anne's cross continued, but overnight she had summoned her courage and fortitude and Cooper was now unable to rattle her. She told him that discrepancies in the police report and her later testimony were due to her now being more fluent in English and having time to think about the events.

Barbara's twelve year old daughter Patti took the stand and her testimony supported Marie Anne's timeline of events.

Patti told the court that Marie Anne ran and stopped at her bedroom door and yelled for her to come out. She jumped out of bed and ran down the hallway, trailing her. Marie Anne exited the lanai door to the home, but Patti stopped short for a moment, then ran out. Marie Anne told her to go back inside and lock the door. Instead, she continued on to the garage. Patti stopped short in front of the closed side door. She heard the brutality taking place inside the garage and scared, ran back into the house and locked the lanai door. She looked through a window in the direction of the garage and heard a shot. She saw Marie Anne coming back and unlocked the door, letting her in. She did not hear the second shot Marie Anne claimed she heard just before entering the home, but she may have confused the time of the shot with Marie Anne's arrival. She may have heard the *second* shot, but not the first which Finch fired in the garage when Marie Anne was there. *Or* she may have heard the shot fired in the garage but not the second because she was already further into the home after opening the door for Marie Anne who heard it outside as she was entering.

Whatever the sequence of events, it was all too traumatic to tell for Patti, who was still in shock over losing her mother to such a violent death at their home. Patti, as Marie Anne also testified, never saw anyone on the lawn nor in the bushes after Marie Anne called police and they waited outside to avoid being shot in the house by Finch. Consequently, their testimony did not support Carole's story of hiding in the bushes for hours before leaving the scene.

The next day, Cooper finally admitted that the prosecution's so-called murder kit was Dr. Finch's and that the contents were also his, including .38-caliber bullets, which lead reporters to speculate that Cooper would introduce the gun that killed Barbara. Cooper was looking forward to questioning Detective Ryan about contradictions in Marie Anne's report to him and Detective Hopkinson the night of the murder, her Finch hearing, and court testimonies, but Ryan was allegedly home sick with the flu.

In his place, West Covina Police Officer Frank Meehan testified about how the police came to be in possession of the attaché case. He arrived on scene about 11:45 the night of the murder and stayed until 2:30 p.m. the next day. He then contradicted Raymond's account of finding the case and holding it for a few days before delivering it to police. He claimed Raymond pointed out the case to him the morning following the murder, at 6:30 a.m., which inferred that as soon as Raymond rose, he ran out directly

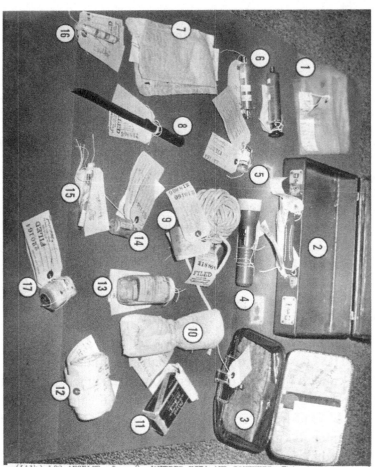

*The murder kit and its contents numbered
and listed on a press photo.*

to the case on the lawn and then to Meehan to alert him to its location. Meehan's claim that he arrived about 11:45 was also suspect. By saying he arrived on the quarter hour, he remarkably placed himself at the murder scene no later than after it happened and, possibly, even before. Meehan appeared to be setting up a timeframe as cover for the police department, particularly the amount of time the attaché case sat on the lawn unattended and unfound by officers who did not thoroughly search the area the night of the murder.

Also unusual for claiming to be the one who first picked up the case, Meehan could not remember if it was wet with dew, sprinkler water or dry. But since it was summer, he *assumed* that it was dry and the defense did not object to his hearsay to establish that he may have been lying about finding the case as the sun rose. Meehan then claimed he brought the case into the lanai, opened it and looked at its contents. But how did he open the case without the necessary key to do so?

It was likely from Meehan's testimony and Captain Ryan's absence in court that day that West Covina Police did not want to have Captain Ryan take the witness stand and be forced to tell the truth and besmirch his and the department's good names. But if Meehan was caught lying, the department would only likely have to reprimand, and possibly fire, a lowly officer and not the police captain. It was all about damage control. There was no way for me to confirm what I believe happened, based on available reports. West Covina Police denied my requests to see its microfilmed files.

The following Monday, Los Angeles County Coroner Dr. Gerald K. Ridge was questioned by Whichello about the location of Barbara's death. He told the court that she was shot close to or at the bottom of the steps leading down to her in-laws' yard. "Her ability to travel after the gunshot wound would be limited to a few steps. It is difficult to believe she could have reached the bottom" after having been shot on the driveway above without falling down the steps. There was no evidence she fell, including any cuts to her knees. Based on Ridge's testimony it was likely that Finch did not shoot Barbara on the driveway as she ran from him. He stopped at the edge of the driveway and shot her as she struggled down the dirt steps to her in-laws' backyard with two skull fractures while wearing just one high heel.

Ridge added that the third skull fracture Barbara received may have occurred during her fall, after she had been shot and killed in the yard, if she hit her head as the body fell on an iron stake used to tie down a tree. It would explain the fact that there was no post-mortem bleeding on that area of her head.

Ridge was questioned about the probable use of the items in the Finch attaché case by Cooper. He said that when taken individually, the items were innocent but that collectively, they were not something a doctor would carry.

Detective Ryan, apparently now recovered from the "flu," finally appeared as a witness. But instead of being questioned about the attaché case, he referred to his notes that said Marie Anne heard "shots" before entering the garage, but testified that she didn't. Whichello asked if, through her Swedish-accented English, she could have actually said "shouts." He agreed, but Grant Cooper objected, which was sustained. Ryan confirmed the location of Barbara's body in photographs and the evidence gathered, including blood smears on the car's front seats. He testified that police did not search around the house or garage, which left the attaché case to be found the next morning by Raymond Finch, and Sergeant Handrahan told him the windows were up on the Chrysler and the radio had been on before he arrived.

Most interesting during Ryan's testimony, he refuted Officer Frank Meehan's claim from the previous week that he was the first one to open the attaché case—*before* police had the key. Ryan recalled being given the key by Las Vegas sheriffs while he was there to escort Finch back to West

Covina. Ryan demonstrated how the key opened the attaché case in court for everyone to see.

CHAPTER 27 – THERAPY

On Tuesday, Barbara's defense attorney, Joseph Forno, told the court that when Barbara first visited him in January the previous year, she told him that if Finch came after her at home, she planned to "kick off her high heels" and run next door to her father-in-law's home. Forno added that from January 1959 to a few days before her death that July, Barbara met with him dozens of times. He testified that Barbara told him how her husband would kill her three weeks before her death. She told Forno about Finch's gun and asked if there was any way he could get it away from him. Forno told her he would try.

Barbara told Forno on several occasions that Finch would have her killed or take her out into the desert or up in the mountains himself and kill her, making it look like an accident. She was not going to get into any car with him. If he forced her at their home to make it happen, she was going to get out of the car or run out of her home to her in-laws. Most tellingly, she told Forno that Finch was not going to allow her to tie up their assets, stocks, and income from the medical center by conceding to her court-ordered control.

After initially meeting with her the previous January, Forno told the court Barbara's divorce was filed the following May 20. After the parties met on June 11 regarding a reconciliation that Finch wanted, Barbara told Forno that Finch's wanting to get back together was just a trick so that he could get her back in the house to kill her. A restraining order was taken out against him, which was supposed to prevent Finch from contacting her, or disposing of community property, and withdrawing funds except as required for business or support. He broke into the house on June 25 and threatened to kill her and beat her up again. Forno prepared an order for contempt of court. The conciliation court date was then put on hold so the contempt action could be dealt with. If conciliation happened as originally scheduled, it would have taken place on July 23, but Barbara was killed on July 18.

On cross-examination, Forno told Cooper that the single man Barbara was out to dinner with at Kelly's Steakhouse the night she died was his law clerk and investigator, Herbert Adair. Forno wanted Barbara to hire a bodyguard but she couldn't afford one with the Finch finances tied up by the court order. Cooper tried to concoct a romantic relationship between the tall, dark-haired Adair and Barbara by way of their mutual membership at the Los Angeles Tennis Club and get Forno to confirm it.

If only.

"If Adair had taken her home from dinner that night, things might have been different," Forno sadly regretted.

Next on the witness stand, Barbara's friend, Marca Helfrich, recalled how Barbara sought asylum from Finch at her Hollywood apartment and recounted the death threats and beatings by Finch. The content of her testimony was not humorous, but her delivery which was often confused about judicial protocol and accented with gratuitous sighs, caused spectators to laugh. Dorothy Kilgallen described Marca in her column that day as "shy and nervous, but she is also very hard to shut up once she starts answering a question. And she has an air of utter honesty."

Whichello asked Marca about Barbara's relationship with Finch. "And do you know what it was she was afraid of?"

"Of course... her *husband!*" Marca looked up at Whichello as though he were an idiot. She paused a beat, sighed, and then added, "Well, he had beaten her up and she was afraid he was going to kill her."

After her testimony, Marca fled the courtroom to avoid reporters and photographers. Cooper looked up after her and in mock resignation made a brow-mopping gesture, smiled, and said, "Well, when my turn comes I don't think I can treat her in [such a] fatherly fashion."

Minnette Haber, the Finches' friend who lived in Palm Springs, was the last to take the stand. She recounted Barbara telling her on the phone in mid-May 1959 that she and Finch had a physical argument, she fell, hit her head, possibly on the bed, and passed out. When Barbara came to, Finch had restrained her and said he was going to put her in the car and run her over a cliff. Barbara told Finch, "Don't do this, Bernie. If you kill me, you will get the gas chamber… and what will happen to Raymie? Who will take care of him?"

CHAPTER 28 – INTERSECTING TRIANGLES

The Asian Flu hit Los Angeles County with a vengeance in January 1960, with abnormally high scores of workers and students. An estimated half million people called in sick across the Southland. The Finch-Tregoff trial was delayed initially on the 13th for five days, but when older juror Floyd G. Jones's flu turned into bronchial pneumonia and he was hospitalized, he was permanently replaced by alternate juror Margaret Cordiak on January 18. Counsel was not immune from the epidemic; one of Carole's attorneys, Donald Bringgold, was also sick. Even Marilyn Monroe, who had been shooting *Let's Make Love,* suffered, but she managed to do so in the regal splendor of a bungalow at the Beverly Hills Hotel.

Others waiting to get into the trial as spectators were impervious. A bug-resistant three hundred and fifty people brawled in the lobby with each other and deputies in the "circus room" to get a spectator's seat. In the process, they knocked over heavy, three foot-high cigarette ash cans and rope stands that had previously kept them at bay. For those one hundred unlucky souls who didn't get in, they had to go to the back of the line and stew about their misfortune of not getting a seat for the morning session.

In court, Finch and Carole's three apartment managers testified. Mrs. Gere Snyder confirmed that she rented an apartment to Finch in Las Vegas at 419 Desert Inn Road. He paid a hundred dollar deposit for the one hundred and seventy-five dollar per month apartment on July 8, 1959, telling Mrs. Snyder that the apartment was for "his fiancé." Mrs. Snyder then described the comings and goings of the police as they rousted Finch from sleep in the bed at 10:30 a.m. on July 19 to arrest him, and then came back about ninety minutes later to speak to Carole, who had now replaced Finch, sleeping in the same bed.

Irma Kelpein, of 442 El Mercado Avenue, Monterey Park, who first rented Finch and Carole an apartment from June 15, 1957, until July 15, 1958, told the court, "At the time, he told me they were going to leave he said they had enjoyed the apartment very much." The court erupted in laughter as Finch folded his arms and grinned broadly. A small, sly smile cracked over Carole's lips. Finch and Carole stayed at a nicer place that was larger and had carpeting in Marcel Goldfarb's building at 215 S. Ramona Boulevard, also in Monterey Park, from July 23, 1958, to July 1, 1959. Dorothy Kilgallen would write about Carole sharing apartments with Finch in her column the next day. "[It] was naughty of her but not a capital offense."

Herald-Express guest columnist and wife of actor James Mason, Pamela Mason cattily fixated on Carole's weight gain from the starchy, high-carb jail food and offered her own medical opinion as to its cause.

Carole Tregoff...looks to be rather blown up, not plump in a cushioned, satisfactory fashion but an unhealthy looking plump body she has on her at the moment. Somebody told me that she has a thyroid condition and has gained thirty pounds since the trial began, however I would say that more likely she is ill, breaking down under the strain imposed upon her and as a result, probably has developed some kind of fluid retention.

At any rate I am sure that she is heavier than she should be, for her face is quite drawn and piqued and her color very grey. She looks unhealthy, unwell and extremely nervous, although she handles herself well and doesn't fidget.

Could Pamela have been jealous of the much younger and attractive Carole? I'd almost forgotten what a shrew she was on talk shows during the 1960s, but Merv Griffin loved her for it and she appeared multiple times on his talk show. Later in the day, Pamela had her photograph taken with Finch. "I hope that you're going to look tougher than I do in this picture," she told him as the photo op was set up. "I don't want to look the villain in this."

"I don't want to look the villain either," Finch retorted.

The real work in the courtroom that day began with the defense attorneys using every legal precedent they could to keep Finch and Carole's three co-conspirators off the witness stand, even claiming at one point they hadn't been given proper legal counseling to keep them from self-incrimination. Failing to scare the street-smart hardened two (Jack Cody had already cut a deal with prosecutors), the third, childhood friend Donald Williams, nervously stepped up to the stand to testify.

Don, petrified, could barely be heard over the PA system and the microphone had to be adjusted to amplify his voice. "He gulped for breath, he twisted his hands, he searched for words, and he dangled his participles. His testimony was hard to take down because he almost never made a sentence with a subject and a predicate. He talked in nervous phrases," Kilgallen wrote. Still, when taken as a whole, those broken sentences with dangled participles added up to one damning story against Carole seeking a low-rent contract killer to clear the path for her to the top of Lark Hill Drive.

Richard Keachie, Williams' philosophy classmate at the UNLV, told the court he saw Carole and Jack Cody (who introduced them) together on two occasions, once at Foxy's restaurant and the other at the Frontier Hotel. In mid-July

1959, Keachie and Cody left Las Vegas for Minneapolis. Keachie returned with two girls, Peggy Bates and Katherine Brombach. Crail asked Keachie if he ever went to the police about the murder plot.

"No."

"They came to you?"

The courtroom erupted in laughter, which continued.

"We sort of met on mutual ground. I was in jail."

Earlier, during the middle of Don Williams' testimony and due to an unexpected break in actor/director Mark Stevens' film schedule, Williams was bumped from the stand and Stevens took his place. Stevens told the court that about seven to ten days before she died, he and Barbara were in the upstairs bar at the Los Angeles Tennis Club. Barbara told him Finch had threatened her life many times and she was afraid that he would kill her. She was "as emotionally upset as anyone I've ever seen," Stevens told prosecutor Crail, but the remark was stricken from the record at Cooper's request. Stevens suggested that Barbara acquire a gun for protection. "I told her I would be happy to show her how to load it and how to use it. I was quite insistent on this, but she refused. I tried to force the issue several times. Each time she said she would be scared to death… and reiterated that she had never even handled a gun.

"I finally went down to her car with her… and got a jack handle out of the back of the car. I told her to keep that in the car and take it in the house with her, and if he came near her to say hello and hit him in the face with it." It happened to be a statement similar to those Stevens had said a number of times as an actor in *films noir*.

Cooper tried to have Stevens' testimony about the jack handle stricken as hearsay but Crail avowed to have further evidence supporting it. Judge Evans partially sided with Cooper by striking Stevens' testimony about the jack, but also reminded the jury that Stevens' testimony should only be considered for showing Barbara's state of mind.

Stevens may have wanted to rethink his appearance in court that day. Minutes before he entered the courtroom, he was met with a subpoena to appear in municipal court. Apparently, he had skipped out on a $537 bill (almost five thousand dollars in 2020) at the Villa Capri Restaurant in Hollywood.

It must have been some pizza party.

CHAPTER 29 – LADY KILLER CODY

Also testifying January 18 was the most important of the three Finch-Tregoff conspirators: John Patrick "Jack" Cody. Of the three men, Cody was the one who had allegedly been paid by Finch and Carole to commit Barbara's murder. The defense attorneys, to the contrary, would argue that Cody was paid as an investigator to discover any affairs Barbara may have been involved in. Dressed in a too-long black suit coat and pants, a white shirt, and tie, Cody was described by the press as though he just stepped off the stage for a community production of *Guys and Dolls*. Full of Damon Runyon swagger and "I says," Cody repeated his grand jury testimony while Carole shot dagger eyes at him. A far change from just six months earlier when they cozied up to each other, haggling over a price to kill Barbara.

Whichello: How much money was mentioned?

Cody: Williams quoted me a price of $2,000.

Whichello: Did [Carole] tell you what it was all about?

Cody: Yes, she wanted me to kill Mrs. Finch.

Whichello: What did she say about the money?

Cody: She said, "That's too much," and I told her… not too much for killing somebody. She said, "Well a thousand dollars was more what I had in mind."

Whichello: You dickered?

Cody: Yes, I told her I needed $100 for a weapon, $100 for a car to approach the Finch home, and some expense money, all of which added up to $1,400. She was to give me $350 down and the balance when I'm through.

Whichello: Did you intend to kill anybody?

Cody: No, sir!

Whichello: Or intend to harm anyone?

Cody: There was no question in my mind. I wasn't going to do it. That's all.

`**Whichello**: What was your purpose in this?

Cody: To get the money.

* * *

Whichello: Was there any other conversation?

Cody: I asked Carole, "Are you sure you want to go through with this?" She said, "Definitely." I told her, "Carole, when I get on that plane, you can't recall me." She said, "Good. Good luck. Everything's fine."

Whichello: What did you do?

Cody: I went in and had another breakfast. I hadn't finished.

Laughter rolled over the courtroom.

* * *

Whichello: Did you see Carole in Las Vegas?

Cody: Yes, about eight that night. She came to my apartment to pay me off… She asked if I had done it. I said, "Yes." She asked me how, and I said "With a shotgun."

Whichello: What else?

Cody: I asked if she had the money and she said, "Yes" and handed me an envelope… $100 bills— oh, seven or eight. I put it in my pocket.

Whichello: Did she express how she felt?

Cody: She was smiling. She was happy. First time I ever saw the girl happy.

The next night he saw Carole in a café and she wasn't smiling. She wanted Cody to confirm that he had shot Barbara.

Cody: I said I'd taken pictures of the woman I shot, after I…put her in the trunk of the car, and that they'd be in in a day or two… She said, "Are you sure you didn't talk to Mrs. Finch and she gave you a better deal?' I said, "No, I didn't talk to Mrs. Finch. I just shot her!"

The courtroom erupted in laughter.

* * *

Whichello asked how Carole introduced Cody to Finch.

Cody: I dunno. He said, "Just call me Bernie." He asked how I killed Mrs. Finch and I told again how I shot her in the chest with a shotgun.

Whichello: What did Dr. Finch say?

Cody: He said, "I just got through talking to my wife and she is very much alive." I said, "That can't be—I shot her." He said a tragic mistake had been made. I think he assumed it was her girlfriend... He asked if I was willing to go back and do it right. I said, "If I've killed the wrong, woman I will."

Cody discussed additional costs and Finch offered to lend him a shotgun. Whichello asked if he received further instructions.

"He told me to tell her why she was getting it... to tell her, 'This is from Bernie' when I killed her."

Audible gasps were heard from spectators in the courtroom.

* * *

Whichello asked Cody about his reluctance to make a statement to him and Captain Ryan in Minnesota the previous September.

"Do you want to know the truth?" Cody asked.

Whichello laughed "Of course we want to know the truth."

"I was waiting for Dr. Finch to send someone to help me...a lawyer. Then I talked to my lawyer, Paul Fish, and he said I was crazy."

Rexford Eagan cut in. "We'll stipulate to that."

"To what?"

"That he's crazy."

Cooper cross-examined Cody about his work ethic and character, both of which he lacked, but showing no sign of shame and somewhat proud of getting by on his wits, Cody didn't produce the results Cooper tried to engineer. "It gave some pause, even to Cooper, who had seen his sharpest barbs glance off Cody's callousness like birdshot off a tank," noted the *Examiner.*

The next day, Cody was further examined by Cooper. "You gave her some fatherly advice, too? You tried to talk her out of it."

"Well, yes. I think I just told her, 'Carole, are you sure you want to go through with it?'"

"Was that part of your con game, or did you mean it?"

"I meant it," Cody replied.

"But you wanted the money?" Cooper pressed.

Cody's demeanor and response softened. "It wasn't that important.... Not to have that lady killed."

"But *you* weren't going to kill her?"

"No, but somebody was. They had gone that far."

"So, of course, you went to the police."

"I did not. I was on the wanted list. I wish I would have though." Cody again described Carole as "happy" when he told her he had killed Mrs. Finch.

"Aren't you exaggerating just a teeny, weeny bit?" Cooper asked.

"No, I'm trying to tell the truth... she was relaxed, like it was a load off her shoulders. She might have smiled, I guess."

"How else did she express delight?"

Cody explained, "Well, she didn't jump up and down. I think she said she was thrilled."

"You are testifying against a person accused of murder. Did she say she was happy?" Cooper shouted.

"Sir, I don't remember."

"Let me ask you, Mr. Cody, do you have any regard for the truth?"

"Yes. Uh-huh."

"But you have no compunction about telling lies, do you?"

"Well, it depends on who I'm dealing with."

"Are you in the habit of discussing murders?" Cooper asked.

"Well, I would occasionally talk about it with people."

"Were you interested in committing a murder at that time?

"No," Cody answered.

"Were you interested in committing a holdup at that time?"

"Yes."

"A burglary?"

"Yes."

"Do you have a way with the girls?"

"I hope so."

"As far as Dr. Finch and Carole Tregoff were concerned, you never at any time had any intention of committing a murder?"

"Yes, that's right." Cody confirmed.

"What did you have to gain by telling this story?"

"Gain? Why nothing."

"You wanted to cooperate with law enforcement officers?"

"Yes."

"Out of the goodness of your heart?"

"No. On the advice of my attorney."

There was laughter in the courtroom.

During a recess, Cody dressed in what he considered natty attire showed off his French cuffs with his name, John, embroidered on them in black. "My own idea," he tapped his forehead. "Class!" He told reporters that he and Carole spent time in various bars, hugging and kissing, and that Finch was jealous of the time she spent with him.

Now, Carole Tregoff was *his* girlfriend.

Cody continued his testimony the next morning. He recounted for Cooper Finch telling him that if he were ever on the lam, he would put him up in his medical clinic as a patient, to which Cody told Finch then he could inject him with something to get him out of the picture. He told Finch he'd just as soon stay out of the clinic, to which they both laughed.

Eagan asked Cody, "Would you lie for money?"

"Would I lie for money? It looks like I have."

* * *

Cooper asked, "Isn't it true that you were hired to follow Mrs. Finch?"

"No, I wasn't hired to follow her. I was hired to kill her."

Audible gasps were heard from spectators.

CHAPTER 30 – THE SMOKING LETTER

Handwriting expert Donn Mire testified that he believed the three thousand dollar check bearing Barbara's signature was forged by Finch, even after Cooper provided him with thirty-six checks with Finch's signature. Twice during his testimony Mire referred to Barbara Finch as Barbara Graham, the infamous murderer recently executed in the gas chamber, as spectators gasped, Carole shuddered, and Finch fixed him with a cold stare. "Did you say Barbara *Graham*?!" a stunned Crail asked.

"I'm sorry, I meant *Finch*," an embarrassed Mire replied amid courtroom laughter.

The confusion had a base in reality: Mire had testified at Barbara Graham's trial. His faux paus presented an opening for Cooper. He asked Mire if he had ever made a mistake. "Mr. Cooper, I'm fifty-seven years old and made lots of mistakes." The courtroom roared with laughter as spectators recalled Mire's confusion of the two Barbaras. Mire still managed to extricate himself from the hole he fell in.

"I know of no case where I have testified in court and have been proven wrong."

Finch initially gave West Covina Medical Center business manager Bryce Rose the check to cash. Rose took it to the California Bank branch in Covina, where the Finches had their account (which was also the branch where my parents banked). Bank employees, Vice President JD Reed and accounts executive Gladys MacDonald, examined the check and called Finch about his rubber-stamped endorsement on the back; then, satisfied with his explanation, cashed the check. Bryce was given a sealed envelope that oddly contained two one thousand dollar bills and two five hundred dollar bills—large denominations requested by Finch. Currency in such large amounts was usually intended for specific payments, not small, outstanding invoiced bills. Why did Finch request such large denominations? What was he buying?

As with the gun, police hadn't found Barbara's white clutch bag, but prosecution witness Betty Behr confirmed for Whichello that she saw it at Kelly's Steakhouse the night Barbara was killed. Cooper asked how she could be sure. She told him that she had forgotten to bring cigarettes with her and asked Barbara if she had any when they were at the restaurant. Barbara reached into the 8x12 clutch for a pack and gave it to Betty, who, fishing for a single one, accidentally dumped half the cigarettes out of the pack. Cooper tried to call into question her memory by asking if she had ever seen Barbara smoke. "I couldn't say exactly," she answered, adding, "maybe they were Mr. Adair's." Betty also remembered the clutch because Adair forgot his wallet and Barbara handed him her purse to pay the bar bill.

Detective Ryan dropped a bombshell and admitted to Whichello that Carole was technically under arrest as a material witness in Las Vegas on July 19. He had only found out the previous Friday on a 3 p.m. phone call with Lieutenant Ray Gubser from the Las Vegas Sheriff's Department. Gubser had told Carole if she didn't wait for West Covina Police, she would be booked as a material witness. It now appeared that it was a ploy on Gubser's part to keep her in custody without arresting her, even though she had dictated and signed a statement. Whichello got Gubser to admit that Carole was not handcuffed at any time nor was she ever placed in a holding cell. She had made her statement voluntarily, sat in Gubser's office, and was not booked for any involvement in Barbara's death.

Carole's defense team was going to wring every last civil rights violation drop from Ryan's testimony that it could, claiming that she was under arrest in Las Vegas. "We had a break today and we are going to pursue it for all we are worth," Rex Eagan told the *San Gabriel Valley Tribune*. With her hair now two shades a darker auburn, a jubilant Carole smiled at her good fortune. Co-counsel Robert Neeb would try to get Carole's murder indictment dismissed on February 1 due to Ryan's admission and the incriminating testimony she gave, known as Exhibit 60, at the Finch hearing in West Covina, which contradicted her Las Vegas statement by claiming her civil rights were violated.

The prosecution made a case for Finch setting a Fourth of July weekend alibi with a La Jolla doubles match with his minister friend and partner, Alan Cheesebro, who, a few weeks later would officiate at Barbara's funeral service in West Covina and at her burial site in Glendora. Lieutenant Gubser testified about arresting Dr. Finch while he was sleeping in Carole's apartment and then coming back later for her. Just as with Finch previously at the apartment, they had to be let in by the landlady and roust Carole from sleep. They wanted to speak to her at headquarters and she agreed. They asked if they could search the place and take Finch's belongings, to which she agreed. They gave her time to get dressed with help of the landlady, who borrowed one of Finch's coats since there were few of Carole's belongings in the apartment. The detectives left with Carole, and Finch's personal things.

At the sheriff's department, Carole told Gubser that she had been with Dr. Finch in West Covina. He told her she was being held technically under arrest as a material witness until West Covina Police arrived. She wanted to see Finch but he told her to wait until West Covina Police arrived, and they did about 8 p.m. In the meantime, she made a statement to sheriffs, was not booked, and eventually taken home, arriving around 10:30 or 11 p.m. the night of July 19.

Sergeant William Hanrahan testified about arriving at the Finch home the night of the murder and the state of the Chrysler in the garage: the keys in the ignition, the radio on, and the windows rolled up. Detective Fred Jolly described the contents of Finch's white Cadillac when it was impounded after the murder at Los Angeles International Airport. Inside the car were a shotgun and receipts for the two Monterey Park apartments made out to a "G. Evans."

"Hired Killer Letter Rocks Finch Trial" headlined the next morning's edition of the *Los Angeles Examiner*. There was good reason for it: Marie Anne had dropped the second bombshell of the previous day.

Grant Cooper recalled Marie Anne to the witness stand to continue to impeach her story of Finch's physical abuse of Barbara. He led her to testify that Barbara had received phone calls the day of the shooting from Finch from Las Vegas and Barstow while he and Carole were on the road to West Covina. In her previous testimony, Marie Anne remembered no such phone calls. During his turn at bat, Crail reminded her about a conversation she had with Barbara on May 18 about Finch threatening to murder her.

"Are you sure she mentioned…a man from Las Vegas?"

"Yes."

"Do you have any reason for remembering?"

"Yes, I had written it down."

"Where?"

"I wrote it about a week after it happened… in a letter to my mother… Her name is Mrs. Anna Lisa Lidholm, and she lives in Gothenburg, Sweden."

Crail produced the letter inside an envelope with a West Covina postmark dated May 25, 1959, a canceled stamp, and an English translation as evidence. Although Cooper objected to entering the contents of the letter, Crail requested Judge Evans read the letter for himself to decide. Evans retired to his chambers with all three legal teams in tow and read Marie Anne's translated letter to her mother in front of counsel.

> During the night, Dr. Finch tried to kill Mrs. Finch, who now absolutely wants to have her divorce. Mrs. Finch told me everything in the morning. He had hit her and she had fallen against the corner of the bedside table and had a deep cut on her temple. He had then tried to make her dress and get her out and into the car, which he threatened to drive over the ridge up by the garage where there is an abrupt descent... He also told her that if she did not take everything back about the divorce he had a man in Las Vegas who he would pay thousands of dollars to kill her.

Cooper vigorously objected to the jury hearing the contents of the letter and Evans agreed, with an exception: the last sentence of Marie Anne's letter would be allowed but to tell jurors the statement was not evidence of the truth but to refute Cooper's claim that Marie Anne had lied during her previous testimony.

Unfortunately for Cooper, Evans had let the genie out of the bottle. The jury heard the last sentence in court. And, it was the most damning.

In addition to Finch stating he would hire a killer to do away with Barbara, he had also stated how much he was willing to pay. Interestingly, he inflated the amount he actually did pay, to impress upon her the length he would go to shut her up. In the end, Finch was just too cheap to pay the amount to have the job done correctly by a professional killer. Or it may have been because he dared not forge the check for a much larger amount, which would have raised suspicion—not only with bank personnel but Barbara. Still, there was a bright side for Finch.

Fortunately, Barbara had not said anything to Marie Anne about being hit with a gun by Finch and there was no reference in her letter to him having done so. Marie Anne's testimony, supported by the letter, flew in the face of the defense's earlier strategy when Cooper tried to discredit her. Now Cooper had to admit she had told the truth.

He also had to figure a way to work around it.

CHAPTER 31 – POPCORN, PEANUTS & THE HOTTEST TICKET IN TOWN

Three weeks into the trial, the only four crimes anyone could be sure that Finch had committed were:

1. grand theft auto for stealing two cars;

2. created false evidence of his wife's affair;

3. ignored his Hippocratic oath by withholding medical treatment for Barbara after she was shot and liable for malpractice prosecution; and

4. check forgery by signing Barbara's name.

Nonetheless, a January 26 *Los Angeles Times* article called the Finch-Tregoff trial the hottest ticket in town for what it *might* expose. People stood in line as early as 6 a.m. and sold their places to others, mostly retirees, less patient, for as high as ten dollars (in 2020, approximately ninety dollars). The *Times* titled the show *Call Me Bernie*.

"I find it's like reading a book. You can't stop until you get to the end," a retired bus driver told the *Times*.

The line to get in started at the Hill Street entrance and snaked around the block. Doors finally opened at seven and there was a rush of people, pushing and shoving to get into lobby elevators to the second floor.

"Some people get away with murder!" an elderly woman exclaimed about a large man who snuck into the line towards the Metropolitan Courthouse, oblivious to the potential double meaning of her statement. Spectators had their favorites in "the cast"—among them, Dr. Finch, Carole, and Grant Cooper, who was known for warming up to witnesses and then "coming in for the hammerlock" when he wasn't incessantly chewing on his glasses.

While waiting for the bailiff to call court to order, Finch was asked by a reporter about playing tennis at the famous celebrity-anointed Racquet Club in Palm Springs, owned by *Seventh Heaven* matinee idol and *My Little Margie* television actor Charles Farrell.

"Oh, yes, we won their last invitational double tournament. I played with a friend. Give my regards to Charlie when you see him."

Seventy-six year old Judge Albert Miller, after recovering from bronchial pneumonia brought on by the Asian Flu the previous week, gave his homespun version of Carole's questioning at Finch's hearing and privately in his chambers during a recess the previous July. He warmly colored his testimony, spicing it with homilies and humor reminiscent of the short story/radio/film homespun character Scattergood Baines, as though he was working the floor of a nightclub or television audience. Courtroom spectators similarly rewarded him with laughter.

At one point, Miller referred to Carole as "Olga," to which Clifford Crail questioned the name.

"I didn't know her name at the preliminary, and I never did learn it. It's my custom to call good-looking girls 'my girl,'" he explained. He added that due to his age, he got away with it. Miller summed up his courtroom philosophy as wanting "to put people at ease and to be at ease myself in my courtroom."

Next, Cooper and Eagan tag-teamed him in a losing cross-examination, objecting every time he veered off course in answering questions, but they were no match for the wily jurist. At one point, Miller was asked about the Finch hearing transcript.

"I never had a copy of the transcript and I wouldn't have had time to read it if I did."

Even Crail found Miller a difficult fish to reel in. "What did you say to her [Carole] after you went into chambers?"

"Well, you haven't—maybe on purpose—inquired as to the occasion of my going into chambers."

Crail was irked. "We've got you in *there*, now we want to know *what* took place."

"I walked in and said to her, 'Now, young lady, here we are. You have been invited into Court chambers as guest of the Court.'"

Miller proved to be so popular that during a recess, photographers ran up to the witness stand where he held court. He smoked his pipe with a large "no smoking" sign on the wall behind him. One of the reporters pointed out that there was no smoking in the courtroom. Over the still-open microphone, Judge Miller roared, "The fuck it is. I didn't see any 'no smoking' signs. Come out to West Covina and I'll show you how to run a courtroom."

Gladys Tregoff, Carole's stepmother, whose age was misreported too much in her favor, took the witness stand. Gladys broke down, bursting into tears, recounting her daughter on the stand during the Finch hearing in West Covina when she was asked whether she had sexual relations with him. A recess was called as Gladys was led away by Carole's attorney Donald Bringgold to an anteroom to recover, just like her stepdaughter at the hearing.

Finch and Carole, both with red, tearful eyes, joined Gladys, where Carole reiterated her stepmother's request that photographers stop taking photos of her sobbing, demanding, "Come on, get out!"

As the reporters and photographers filed out, the last one, TV photojournalist Ed Clark, turned around to get one last picture. Finch, standing nearby, swung his cuffed hands sideways, landing a soft punch in Clark's stomach.

After the short recess, Bringgold asked a now composed black-suited, pink-gloved Gladys what Judge Miller said in his chambers. Gladys did not hear him say that Carole didn't have to answer the question about sexual relations put to her on the stand. The judge excused the jury so attorneys, including Robert Neeb, could argue whether Carole's testimony at the Finch hearing could be admitted as evidence.

It would take Neeb over ninety minutes to make his case.

Carole's attorney, Robert Neeb shows her the pleading he used to prohibit Exhibit 60, her Finch hearing testimony, from being used as evidence against her at the trial.

CHAPTER 32 – THE HOT SEAT, PART I

On February 2, with the jury momentarily removed, Judge Evans ruled that Carole's testimony in the pre-trial hearing, her knowledge of Finch's intentions while she placed the murder kit in her car trunk, known as Exhibit 60, was inadmissible because she was not advised that it could be used against her in a criminal action. There were audible sighs and a multiple "oh, no!"s from spectators. Her attorney Robert Neeb now felt emboldened.

"This young lady has immunity and cannot, as a matter of law, be prosecuted in this court."

"Is counsel making a *motion* to that effect? Evans asked.

"Yes."

"That motion will be denied—or overruled," declared Judge Evans.

Evans allowed Carole's statements to West Covina and Las Vegas police to be admitted. Photos were published of a smiling Carole with Robert Neeb holding his mile-long typed notes he used to plead against admission of Exhibit 60. Carole kissed Neeb on the cheek. Her hairdo was also in a celebratory mood. She was sporting a new bouffant, which, if it was new according to her, occurred by accident she told reporters. She had been doing her own hair since she was a child. "These curlers speak for themselves" she told them as she came from her cell to the jailer commander's office in curlers and a scarf, turban style, before getting ready to enter court.

Gladys was also happy although it was hard to tell. "We just have to win some time!" she stammered through her tears to reporters.

CHAPTER 33 – CAROLE'S STATEMENT TO LAS VEGAS SHERIFFS

On Friday evening, July 17, while working at the Sands hotel, I received a long distance call from Dr. Finch in West Covina, Calif. He advised me that he did not have to work Saturday, July 18, and therefore to meet him at McCarran Airport at 11:30 Friday night.

I picked him up at 11:30 p.m. We then went and had dinner and two drinks at the Sands hotel. We stayed there until approximately 2 or 3 a.m., then we went to my apartment at the above address.

The following morning, I went to work at 10 a.m., and at 6 p.m. the same day, July 18, we left for Los Angeles and arrived in West Covina at approximately 10 to 10:30 p.m. We immediately went to the residence of Mrs. Finch and waited on the lawn for her to come home.

She arrived about five minutes later and we met her in the garage. When Mrs. Finch saw us, she screamed or hollered and got out of her car. An attempt was made to talk to her without success. She then reached into the car somewhere and brought out a gun which she pointed at me. At that instant, Dr. Finch jumped to remove it from her possession and I ran from the garage.

Las Vegas Sheriff's detectives questioned Carole.

Q: *Where did you run to when you left the garage?*

A: I ran into some shrubbery that surrounded the house.

Q: *Where was Mrs. Finch when you left the garage?*

A: I don't know.

Q: *Where was Dr. Finch?*

A: He was standing near my left side.

Q: *Was he standing near Mrs. Finch?*

A: Probably within four or five feet.

Q: *Why did you and Dr. Finch go to Los Angeles in your car?*

A: First of all, he didn't have his car. Therefore we drove down in my car to talk to her. Previously, he had wanted me to go with him, so we could both talk to her and get things straightened out. This time I had agreed to his wishes.

Q: *What was it that you and Dr. Finch wanted to get straightened out?*

A: In going through their divorce. She was trying to make it hard as she could; therefore interfering with his work.

Q: *To your knowledge, had Mrs. Finch applied for a divorce?*

A: She had.

Q: *Had you ever seen Mrs. Finch prior to last night?*

A: Yes, at social occasions, at her home and at my previous employment.

Q: *How long have you known Dr. Finch?*

A: Four and one half years.

Q: *When did you start going with him?*

A: Two and one half years ago.

Q: *Since you have been going with Dr. Finch, has he helped support you?*

A: He has given me money, when I needed it, but has never supported me.

Q: *After you ran from the garage last night, did you hear anything like a gun being fired?*

A: Once, maybe twice.

Q: *Did you see Mrs. Finch's housekeeper at any time?*

A: No.

Q: *Did you see Dr. Finch (unintelligible) when he [left the] house or garage?*

A: No.

Q: *How long did you stay in the shrubbery surrounding the house?*

A: Approximately six hours.

Q: *Did you hear any cars leave the residence while you were there?*

A: Many police cars coming and going.

Q: *Where did you go after you left the area of Mrs. Finch's residence?*

A: Las Vegas.

Q: *In your car?*

A: That's right.

Q: *What time did you arrive in Las Vegas this morning?*

A: Nine o'clock.

Q: *Did you see Dr. Finch after you arrived in Las Vegas this morning?*

A: When I came home he was in bed. We talked some, however he was fuzzy about details and appeared not to know the actual outcome. I then got ready for work and left at 10 a.m.

Q: *Did Dr. Finch tell you how he returned from West Covina to Las Vegas this morning?*

A: He said he had driven, however he wasn't sure how he had obtained a car, but said that he had probably stolen it, but didn't know from whom or where.

Q: *At any time since you've known Dr. Finch have you ever seen him in possession of a firearm?*

A: Yes.

Q: *Do you know what kind?*

A: No.

Q: *Were you and Dr. Finch planning on getting married after he obtained his divorce?*

A: Yes.

Q: *Did you leave Los Angeles and come to Las Vegas because of trouble with Mrs. Finch or for other reasons?*

A: Dr. Finch thought perhaps I might be subpoenaed as correspondent [sic] in her divorce action.

CHAPTER 34 – DRAMA QUEEN

Disgraced former Los Angeles Police Department psychiatric consultant J. Paul de River composited the left and right sides of Finch's face with their respective mirror images into two new portraits—one with both sides left and the other with both right—to create his clinical impression of Finch's mind in an article headlined "The Two Faces of Dr. Finch" for the *Herald-Express*. de River which he purposely pronounced *de-rye-ver* and whose real name was Paul Israel, had been creating these depth psychology portraits for over a decade for the paper, but his dubious past of unsubstantiated employment at elite medical schools and advocating lobotomy as a "cure" for homosexuality left his analysis of Dr. Finch suspect.

Based on de River's illustration and interpretation, the left side, the private side people hide from others, of Finch's face said that he was insecure and his outward aggression compensated for a feeling of inferiority. Finch's actions were based on his emotions and not rational thought processes. He took what he felt belonged to him, no matter the cost. His mouth expressed sensuality and determination. The right side, the public side, revealed him to appear calm and affable, a social country club-loving man. He was intelligent and calculating, but his mouth and eyes expressed a degree of fear.

If one were following the case in the media at the time, they too might have come to the same conclusions about Finch—even without a medical degree from Tulane University.

On February 3, 1960, a drizzle gently blanketed those who began to line up at 3:30 a.m. in front of the Metropolitan Courthouse determined to see the highlight of the trial, Dr. Bernard Finch's testimony, in person. The line outside was calm compared to the one that formed in the lobby after the front doors were opened four hours later. *Ability to Kill* author Eric Ambler, who attended the trial, recalled "the corridor outside the courtroom became packed to suffocation. For once, the air conditioning seemed ineffective. One elderly lady, who fainted in the line, came to as she was being borne away and piped a despairing 'Hold my place.'

"Nobody did."

Inside the courtroom wasn't much better, with spectators who using phony credentials attempted to gain seating in the press section but were ejected by bailiffs. Ambler also noted "a columnist [Dorothy Kilgallen] famed for her appearance on *What's My Line?* was mobbed by autograph hunters. A woman juror got into a violent argument with one of the court [bailiffs] who refused to leave his post to get her book autographed. One cameraman was standing on the judge's desk to get a wider angle on the scene."

Circus Room indeed.

When court was finally called to order, Grant Cooper captivated the courtroom as he outlined Finch's testimony to come. During the course of his opening statement, Cooper made an unintentionally humorous remark, calling into question Finch's medical reputation. "He will explain and tell you that the reason he engaged this apartment under an assumed name was for a several fold purpose... First, he did not want to either embarrass his wife nor did he want others to know that he, an ostensibly reputable physician, did not want it bruited about that he was having this liaison with Carole."

Finch began his long and highly anticipated testimony at 3:20 p.m. "He took the stand with the air of an experienced pilot taking over for an instrument landing in a dense fog—

tense, but steady, nerves well under control," Ambler wrote. Finch was about to play the role of his life, one that he had been preparing for just as long. "He asked at once if he could dispense with the microphone and rely upon the strength of his own voice to carry. 'If you can't hear me,' he instructed Cooper, 'hold up your hand.'"

Having Finch speak directly, without the artificial electronic distortion of the PA system to the jury, may have been a calculated move on Cooper's part; to present him as someone who might be your friendly next-door neighbor out watering his lawn, with whom Cooper was having an over-the-picket-fence conversation.

"I must say it became increasingly more difficult to realize that Dr. Finch was on trial for his life and not someone you had just met at a dinner party," guest reporter and actress Jayne Meadows noted.

Finch played to the jury, summoning his "Call Me Bernie" persona, alternately seducing jurors by making them part of the conversation; when he couldn't remember what kind of concrete was used in making his swimming pool, he looked to them for an answer: "Can anybody help me find the word? I don't remember the word." Or making them laugh, as though jurors were conspirators in his wildly funny, off-color joke at a cocktail party.

But comedy wasn't Finch's only specialty. Just like the two sides of a Greek theatre mask, Finch was also adept at tragedy. When asked by Cooper if the pistol he bought in 1950 was intended to be used to kill Barbara, he replied tearfully, "No."

"Doctor, did you, on the night of July 18, 1959, murder your wife?"

"Absolutely not."

"Or at any other time?"

"No."

"Dr. Finch, did you at any time conspire, combine, confederate, or agree or enter into any kind of a conspiracy with Jack Cody, with Carole Tregoff, or any other living person to kill and murder your wife?

"No, sir, I certainly did not."

Finch related how Carole became his new medical secretary and their romantic relationship began. In November 1956, with the Finches more distant—and Barbara frigid, according to Finch—they had come to an "armistice agreement." According to Finch, they agreed that he would not approach Barbara for sex to maintain peace, but that they would continue to stay married for the sake of the children and to maintain a good line of credit for the two hundred and fifty thousand dollars in loans he and Dr. Gordon were seeking to build West Covina Hospital. Barbara didn't go without reward for her part in this agreement, according to Finch. He gifted her with a modeling course and a new 1957 Cadillac in December to seal the deal.

In July 1957, Finch and Carole were spotted coming out of a supermarket in Monterey Park, hand-in-hand, with a bag of groceries. A car horn honked at them. Finch turned to look. It was Barbara, waving at him from behind the steering wheel of her car. Finch told the court he waved back. Later that evening, when he and Barbara had a conversation about the incident, he told her he was not having a relationship with Carole.

Why would Barbara think Finch would interrupt his day to carry out groceries for Carole?

He didn't do it for Barbara.

Finch tied up some loose ends. Barbara's tears caused the ink on the three thousand dollar check to smear when she signed it, so she made out another and signed it. Mrs. Reida Rands, Finch's previous medical secretary, had resigned for "personal reasons," according to Finch.

What were they?

Was it possible Finch was sexually harassing her? Or making her leave so Carole could replace her?

Cooper felt it was a good time to end on this note and complained to the judge of exhaustion. He asked for a recess until the following day and Judge Evans adjourned court.

The next day, Finch's testimony closely followed Cody's, except that Finch claimed Cody was hired to get evidence on Barbara of an extra-marital affair, not kill her. The first time Cody stiffed Finch and Carole for not producing results of Barbara's affair, Finch allegedly took the high road. "If this guy's pulling a con game, I'm going to make trouble for him. I'll report him to the police," he allegedly promised himself.

Finch identified the attaché case and its contents during Cooper's questioning. It was the first time the defense had acknowledged the so-called murder kit and its contents in court.

Finch recounted setting up Carole in her apartment in Las Vegas, hiring Cody, and his attempts at speaking with Barbara in person. He claimed the gun ended up in the Chrysler (and ultimately in her hand when she threatened him and Carole in the garage the night of her death) when he asked to borrow it from its place in their home to go shark hunting and left it in the car in Newport Beach after returning from Catalina.

Finch's emotional state built as he recounted approaching the house the night of Barbara's death. He claimed Barbara refused to talk to him and Carole and, as he looked at Carole, Barbara pulled a gun on her. He tossed a shaving kit bag, which he had pulled out of the attaché case and contained bullets, to Carole to hold and yelled for her to run. Finch charged at Barbara and they began to struggle over the gun.

When he got to this part, Finch demonstrated by lunging at Cooper, who was standing in for Barbara. Cooper dramatically staggered against the witness stand, startling several female jurors. "Not so hard, doctor, I'm an old man, you know."

Finch recounted a second struggle for the gun in the garage and hearing Marie Anne's footsteps headed towards the garage. Cooper asked Finch why he hit Barbara with the gun.

"Help was coming for her—not me."

How was Finch so sure that it was Marie Anne running out to the garage to help Barbara? And, he claimed, with a rifle, which she wouldn't have had time to assemble and load?

After Barbara and Marie Anne were neutralized and Carole out of danger outside, "a thoughtful jury might wonder why the doctor didn't put the gun in his pocket at that time, dash out of the garage, find Carole, and get away as soon as possible," Kilgallen wrote. "It was quite apparent by then that his wife was not in the proper frame of mind for the reasonable little divorce chat he had come to have with her."

But was the jury paying attention?

Finch moved on, detailing Marie Anne's entrance and involvement, and a third and final struggle with Barbara for the gun before she ran down the driveway in front of her in-laws' home.

She dropped the gun in the struggle and took off, headed down dirt steps onto the front lawn, and Finch picked it up, and as he began to hurl it away, it discharged. Barbara ran down the steps and collapsed on the lawn.

Kilgallen had her say in her column. "Naturally, he dashed down to assist her. He didn't like her and she had been making his life miserable and she certainly had given him a hard time that night, but after all, he's a gentleman and a doctor."

Finch ran to her and cradled her head. "What happened Barbara? Where are you hurt?"

"What was in his mind as he went down the steps? You'd be surprised. He had heard the shot, he had seen the white fire of the bullet right in front of his eyes, but he thought maybe Barbara had broken her leg as stumbled? It never occurred to him that she had been shot? He had to ask her to find out?" Kilgallen asked incredulously.

Finch repeated Barbara's dying words to him. "Shot… in… chest…"

"Don't try to talk, Barb. You stay here real quiet. Don't move a thing. I've got to get you to an ambulance and get you to the hospital."

"Wait…" Barbara moved her hand towards Finch, who took it in his. Her voice was soft.

"I'm sorry… I should have listened…"

"Barb, don't talk about it now. I've got to get you to a hospital."

"Don't leave me… take… care… of… the kids." She went limp. Finch felt for her pulse, but there was none.

"Barb! Barb!"

"Curtain!" Kilgallen called out in her column. "No one could ask for a more dramatic tale than the doctor told on the witness stand. And no one could imagine one more inviting of the slings and arrows of the prosecution."

Finch broke down and cried on the stand, as did Carole at the counsel table, and three women in the jury. Finch was now sobbing and led in handcuffs from the witness stand to an anteroom, blubbering uncontrollably all the way. So were spectators. Most importantly for Finch and Cooper were the women sobbing in the jury box.

Cooper had purposely chosen Friday for Finch's dramatic testimony. Like with any good cliffhanger, the jury—and the public—would have to wait three days with bated breath for the next chapter in the saga of *Call Me Bernie*. In the meantime, Finch's account of the night of Barbara's murder would be the one everyone in the courtroom remembered. It would also be the one the public read about in newspapers or heard on radio and television over the weekend. There would be no other courtroom distractions for three whole days to diminish its impact and prevent it from establishing a beachhead as the truth in the public's mind.

Cooper was counting on that.

On Monday, Finch told reporters that he had been able to recover over the weekend. "The tension of those three days is gone. I'll be all right now," he shamelessly pandered, seeking sympathy—like an actor on a daytime soap opera taking it on the chin and soldiering on after receiving a terminal prognosis from the doctor.

On the stand, Finch picked up where he left off. He recalled going back to the garage after Barbara was shot, sitting down against the Chrysler with its open door, and crying. He noticed the contents of Barbara's purse strewn across the garage floor, along with the purse, where he dumped them. He picked them up and placed the contents back in the purse. He was startled by a noise, which triggered his mind to consider the notion that Barbara may not be dead. He ran back to the scene, but her body was lifeless. The next thing he remembered was running away. He may have had the gun and the purse. Or he may not. He simply couldn't recall.

Cooper interrupted Finch's story to ask him about Barbara's wedding and engagement rings. Did Finch take the rings off her hand? No. Did he see the rings? No.

Nor did police ever find them after searching the home and grounds because Raymond had already removed them, along with the silverware tray where they were hidden.

But how did they end up on the silverware tray to begin with?

Did Barbara place the rings there once she decided she no longer wanted to remain married to Bernie? Or did Finch somehow manage to sneak back into the house to hide the rings after killing Barbara while Marie Anne and Patti were on the front lawn waiting for police?

If he did, was Finch's intent to enter the home have been to kill witnesses?

Finch recalled falling down three times running from Barbara's body (the second time in a plowed field on the South Hills Country Club golf course; the third time in an orange grove where he stayed on the ground to collect himself). He couldn't remember if or where he dropped Barbara's purse and the gun. He told the court he went in and out of conscious memory about events, including his stealing two cars and the driving of the second, coming to the realization he was heading towards Las Vegas. Finch fully regained his senses once he reached city limits and realized he was near Carole's apartment. He confirmed that he arrived at Carole's building at 6:30 in the morning because he had to get the landlady give him a key. His admission implied he was on the road to Las Vegas no later than 1:30 a.m. to make the five-hour drive from West Covina without stopping. It also suggested that there were ninety minutes between the time Barbara died and when Finch ran through the orange grove, stole the two cars, went to his office at the medical center, and gave chase to police at high speeds before doubling back to Sin City.

If there was any doubt that Cooper and Finch hadn't spent a lot of time rehearsing his defense testimony, it should have disappeared when Finch (who couldn't remember major events of the night) recited stolen car owner Carl Mossberg's exact street address.

Finch was cross-examined by Whichello, who started with questions about his practice, financials, and community property laws. The cross led to Finch's other extramarital affairs. Finch said he went out with other "girls" during his marriage to Barbara.

"In both of these instances, is it not true that you told both ladies that you loved them?" Whichello asked.

"Under those circumstances, I think that would be routine."

Spectators in the courtroom laughed. Carole stifled giggles throughout as Finch told about his affairs with her and two other women, referred to in the courtroom as Mrs. X and Miss Y to protect their identities. One of these women, incensed over being dumped by Finch for Carole, ratted him out to Barbara, telling her about his affairs with her and Carole.

Carole may have been smiling Mona Lisa-like at Finch's story, but her demeanor towards him now changed. She did not exchange sly, loving glances with him for the first time. Whichello asked Finch if Barbara approved of the affairs. He also suggested that *they* were the reason for her socalled frigidity and not anything organic emotionally or physically wrong with her as Finch claimed.

Whichello summed up Barbara's state of mind. She just disliked Finch.

Finch told Whichello that he "didn't have any moral values at the time and was free to come and go... And I knew that Barbara wasn't getting any—I don't mean this in a crude way, she wasn't getting any love at home." Finch finally admitted to Whichello that he lied to his wife, the conciliation court, the marriage counselor, his financial advisor, the bank, and his business partner, Dr. Franklin Gordon, who knew, saying he didn't tell him, about the affairs.

The following day there was an intermission in Finch's testimony when Jimmy Pappa took the stand. He denied a sexless life with Carole, refuting Finch's claim. "He is making a mockery of my marriage" the twenty-six year old stated. "I should have given him the beating he deserved when I found out he was going out with Carole ten months before Mrs. Finch's death." Carole had told Jimmy while they were married that Finch had affairs with women at work, who told her she would be next. *The doctor even made eyes at her.*

Jimmy told a CNS reporter that even after she left him for Finch, she was still interested in being in his company. After her release on bail, she called and wanted to go water skiing, but her attorneys thought it was a bad idea and dissuaded her. "But you know, the funny thing about Carole, you'd never know anything was wrong. A woman was dead and she was involved and here she wanted to go water skiing. She acted as if nothing was wrong."

When Finch's testimony resumed, he contradicted himself when he told the court that although Barbara was frigid towards him, that she wouldn't be towards other men. He was counting on it in hope of catching her in an affair, even in the unlikely event that it was with Jack Cody. Whichello asked him if he really thought Barbara would accept a date with Cody.

"She drove a red Chrysler around the Hollywood Hills and she moved in a world of swimming pools and riding academies and expensive restaurants. Afternoons found her lolling around the tennis club with movie stars," Dorothy Kilgallen wrote.

With all this going for her, would Barbara even consider getting in bed with a man whose finesse was as ill-fitting as his suit, even if the shirt cuffs were embroidered with his initials?

Finch claimed Barbara tried to bite him on the arm and knee him in the groin during the struggle for the gun and that she stomped on his feet with her white satin pumps. Whichello asked Finch how he subdued her with the gun.

"May I show you how I did it, sir? If you'll give me the gun, I promise I won't hit you with it," Finch told him.

Whichello agreed and pulled up his pants legs to expose baby blue socks as he sat on the floor. Finch demonstrated the struggle with the gun and how he hit Barbara to disarm her on Whichello, standing in for Barbara.

"I grabbed Barbara's hair" Finch told the court, reaching for Whichello's, but since Whichello was bald this part couldn't be so easily recreated. They moved on with Finch raising the gun above his right ear and bringing it down to within an inch behind Whichello's left ear.

"Surely you could keep it away from Barbara without breaking her skull?" Whichello asked. Finch replied he didn't want to give her any opportunity, especially since he figured that Marie Anne was on her way out to the garage with a shotgun he had previously shown her how to use.

After court adjourned, Finch turned around and told Whichello he kept his promise of not hitting him. "Yes, that was borne out, but I was afraid the temptation might be too great," Whichello quipped.

By the last day of Finch's testimony, Whichello had already been called out by the media for being too soft on Finch during his cross-examination. In her column, Kilgallen wrote that it was about as "effective as a barrage of marshmallows."

"There is something monumentally naive about Prosecutor Whichello's harping on Dr. Finch's little sins, his small deceptions. The picture is apparently quite obvious to everyone in the courtroom except the nice man conducting the cross-examination for the State of California," she concluded.

Whichello's general courtroom behavior may have also played a part in the press's conclusion about his inability to come down hard on Finch.

"He had a habit of mislaying his documents and exhibits. Photograph in hand he would advance on a witness. 'I show you this photograph of a Cadillac car,' he would begin sternly, 'and ask if you can identify...' At that moment, he would himself catch sight of the photograph, realize that it showed a house or a bullet wound, and break off. 'Excuse me, Your Honor,' he would say to the judge, and then pick his way unhurriedly through the contents of a big soap-flakes carton in which he kept his records of the case. If this failed him, he would cross to the courtroom filing cabinet, containing the already-labeled exhibits, and try there. Usually, he found what he wanted in the end, but the delays were boring and gave the prosecution's case an indecisive air," Eric Ambler remembered.

Feeling the heat, not only from the media and the public, but more importantly, District Attorney McKesson, Whichello knew he had one chance left to redeem himself. He finally switched gears.

"Why on Earth didn't you leave them?" he asked Finch, upon his disarming Barbara and subduing Marie Anne. "You still thought you could talk to your wife about a divorce?" Barbara had two concussions from being pistol-whipped. Why hadn't Finch disposed of the gun after Barbara was subdued? Finch had no real answer. Why did Finch not tend to his unconscious wife in the garage?

Finch told him he was standing closer to Marie Anne. Whichello did not question Finch about how his wife could sneak up behind him and clasp her hands over his on the gun without his noticing her approach. Nor did Finch seem believable when he claimed Marie Anne said, "oh no!" in a Kewpie doll-voice as she scampered into the car when the gun accidentally discharged the first time. Whichello did question Finch's reasoning when putting the gun down right next to his bleeding wife as she sat in the car, when she apparently fought so hard to get it from him.

Finch claimed Barbara grabbed the gun and jumped out of the car. He thought she might shoot him so he jumped out of the car on the other side to keep it between them as a buffer. Still, she was "bobbing up and down," trying to line up a shot on him. Unable to do that, she gave up and ran out of the garage. Finch claimed he gave chase because he was afraid she would shoot Carole.

"But you didn't see Carole again?" Whichello asked.

"No."

Probably because Carole was already halfway back to Las Vegas.

Whichello confirmed that Finch's statement to Las Vegas sheriffs was recorded on tape, and although he didn't have it, he did have a transcript and read from that. In his statement to sheriffs, Finch claimed he didn't know his wife was dead, contradicting what he said in court about being with Barbara when she died. Finch was asked if he made up the deathbed scene so that it wouldn't look as though he abandoned a dying woman on the lawn. Finch snapped that was not true. Why hadn't Finch taken her into a neighbor's home? Or his parents', since they were already in their backyard, just feet from an entrance to the home.

Whichello pointed out more discrepancies in Finch's statement with Las Vegas Police, such as his hitchhiking from West Covina instead of stealing the two cars. He asked Finch if he had "an ethical regard of the truth."

"Mr. Whichello, I am fighting for my life and liberty… and also, maybe, for Carole's. The only armament that I have is to tell you folks the truth, and God willing, I will be freed if I keep telling it."

At the end of his testimony, Finch professed his love for Carole and wanted to marry her if she would still have him. Carole and her attorneys—Neeb, Eagan and Bringgold—considered whether she would testify, possibly due to how Whichello finally rose to the occasion and broke apart Finch's defense.

Carole's defense team planned its strategy over Lincoln's birthday, with Gladys providing shrimp cocktails, salad, and Italian pastries for everyone, while Finch and Carole picnicked in the Circus Room. The following Monday, Judge

Evans reprimanded the defense attorneys, who explained it was a lunch meeting between attorneys and clients that couldn't take place in the empty courtroom across the hall because the lights didn't work.

Did they consider candlelight? It would have been more romantic.

*Jimmy Pappa makes an appearance in court as a
spectator and takes a break to bone up on the case. The
newspaper's headline reflects Judge Evans' anger about
Finch and Carole's "picnic" in the courtroom. The two
photographs on the front page are police psychiatrist J.
Paul de River's composite illustrations representing the
two sides of Carole's personality as he interpreted them.
He took the negative, split the image, reversed each half,
and composited them to their respective sides of her
face. De River had earlier done the same for Finch.*

CHAPTER 35 – THE HOT SEAT, PART II

When Dorothy Kilgallen asked one of Carole's attorneys the previous month if she would testify, he laughed. A second attorney told her why.

"After all, she didn't do it," he matter-of-factly stated, as though his word alone was reason enough to set her free. Still, in reality, Carole's attorneys knew it was going to be hard to prove that, although she hadn't fired the gun that killed Barbara, Carole didn't have a major role in the conspiracy to murder her. If conspiracy alone could be proven, there was still a good chance she could end up in the gas chamber. And this was not even considering that she would likely spend the rest of her life behind bars, even if she managed to escape the gas chamber.

To save herself, Carole would now be forced to explain away what others involved in the plot had already connected her to in Barbara's death. Could she claim a possible defense, as Kilgallen suggested, that, being under the intoxicating love of Dr. Finch, her moral center had been clouded?

Could she convince the jury that she was not the femme fatale tabloid magazines like *Hush-Hush* and *On the Q.T.* had portrayed on their covers and pages next to Brigitte Bardot and Jayne Mansfield?

Could she convince the jury that she would abstain from all pleasures of the flesh and devote her life to the poor by joining a nunnery?

"It is hard to imagine her spending an afternoon playing canasta with the girls if she could find anything better to do, and she looks as if she has always been able to find something better to do, and someone to do it with," Kilgallen wrote. It was going to be a tough battle ahead to convince the jury that Carole Tregoff was, if not pious, at least innocent.

Jimmy Pappa unexpectedly appeared in the courtroom as a spectator. Jimmy had come to Superior Court to pick up a copy of his final divorce decree and, since he happened to be in the neighborhood, thought he may as well stop by and see how his ex-wife was doing at her murder trial. Why, what the hey?

"I don't want to see her get the death penalty, but it wouldn't bother me if she got a couple of years—she made a fool out of me," he told reporters turning the story inward on him. When his attention finally returned to Carole, he explained her absences from their home by saying she and Finch were together on house calls. He paused a moment to appreciate the irony.

"I guess they had been at that," he quipped.

Carole began her testimony at 2:32 p.m. She was initially questioned by her lead attorney Robert Neeb for just three minutes. She told him that she did not hire Cody to murder Mrs. Finch, and that she and Finch only went to West Covina to speak to Barbara about a divorce, not murder her.

On cross-exam by Crail, Carole startled spectators when, tearfully, she told the court that she saw Barbara twice with a gun during the night of her death. The first time, when Barbara pointed the gun at her in the garage, and the second, a surprise to the courtroom, just before she ran down the driveway. The latter occurred when Carole looked back and saw Barbara standing briefly behind the car. Crail demanded, "You have never told this before—why didn't you tell it to the police officers?"

"I just forgot about it," she meekly replied.

When asked if she was complicit in Barbara's death, she burst into tears. Unlike Whichello's low-key, non-confrontational cross of Finch, Crail ripped into Carole, causing both sets of attorneys to shout over one another in the courtroom. Crail pointed out contradictions in her testimony with what she told police regarding her knowledge of the so-called murder kit, and her and Finch's intention for seeing Barbara to discuss a divorce. Crail unnerved and confused her to such a point, going back and forth on the timeline of events, that she let down her guard and admitted she had identified the murder kit's contents on the stand during the Finch hearing. A surprising admission that some in the courtroom believed she was now unwittingly giving the prosecution the opportunity to use her entire testimony, Exhibit 60, from the Finch hearing as evidence. But Crail somehow missed the opportunity and asked if she recalled her testimony. Like every accused person acting as the perfect witness for themselves, her memory had conveniently failed her.

"Would you like to have me refresh your memory with the transcript?" Crail asked.

"If you think it is necessary, Mr. Crail," she responded, knowing that he couldn't impeach her with her previous testimony at the hearing.

Crail questioned Carole about why she paused on the lawn to put the shaving kit with bullets in the attaché case if Barbara had the gun and was likely to shoot her after she ran out of the garage. She didn't know. He next asked how long after she left the garage that she heard a gunshot.

"Mr. Crail, I couldn't anywhere near [tell] you how long it was."

"Was it an hour?"

"I'm sure it wasn't."

"A half hour?"

"Mr. Crail, I don't know. I just don't know."

"You can tell time, can't you? I am asking you to give me your best estimate."

"I don't want to try and be wrong."

"Go ahead and we'll tell you whether or not you are wrong."

"Mr. Crail, I would rather not. Because I don't know."

"You are trying to tell the truth here, aren't you?"

"Yes, I am. That is why I am not giving an estimate."

"How many shots did you hear?"

"In the course of the evening?"

"This is the *only* evening we are talking about, so far."

"I think two."

"Weren't you curious about Dr. Finch?"

"I don't think I thought about Dr. Finch."

"Didn't you wonder whether he had been shot?"

"I don't think so."

"Weren't you madly in love with him?"

"I was in love with him."

"Is the word 'madly' too strong? Well, were you in love with him?"

"Yes, sir."

"You thought you were more in love with him than any other man in your life, isn't that correct?"

"I was in love with him… at that time… after what I had seen, I wasn't thinking whether I was in love with anyone."

"He was the most important thing in your life at that time, wasn't he?"

"Apparently not, if I didn't think of him."

"These events were clearer in your mind then than now, seven months later?"

She wanted to explain; Crail wanted answers.

Finch's attorney Grant Cooper jumped in. "I think the witness is confused."

"She has three attorneys sitting here to help her out—just which defendant is Mr. Cooper representing?" Crail demanded.

After getting Carole to admit that she and Barbara did not speak to each other, Crail hammered home her claim she was going to speak to Barbara about getting a quickie divorce in Nevada. "Then you believed she would talk to you, even though she was about to name you as co-respondent in the divorce action?"

Finch suffered in silence for Carole, but was visibly disturbed by her ordeal. Although her defense team later put a happy face on her testimony, others present thought she had hurt herself and, in turn, Finch.

"There was simply too much she could not remember," Dorothy Kilgallen recalled. "There were strange contradictions between what she told police last July when the events surrounding the death of Barbara Jean Finch were fresh in her mind, and what she wants the present jury…to believe."

It all came down to: if Carole was so frightened, enough to run from the garage and allegedly hide in the bougainvillea bush, why did she spend time caching the shaving kit with the bullets before running out and, once outside, take the time to place it in the attaché case?

Why didn't she just run off after she heard the first gunshot fired in the garage?

It was likely that she actually did. Prosecutors had overlooked her comment to a reporter the previous July that she was a block away, racing back to the car, when she heard the second shot.

How did they miss it?

Five days later, on February 20, *Perry Mason* producer Gail Patrick Jackson's research visits to Bernard Finch's trial for program material finally paid off. The episode entitled "The Case of The Wary Wildcatter" aired on CBS in the evening. In the episode, a man pushed a car, with his wife in it, over a cliff. Unlike the Finch case where it was planned but never executed, or the John Robert Briggs case

*An artist's rendition of Carole's dogged
grilling by prosecutor, Clifford Crail.*

where it actually happened, the villain of the story is caught on camera performing the dastardly deed.

The following day, Finch told a reporter if he was acquitted, he hoped to resume his medical practice in West Covina, but cautioned, with the notoriety he has received, he may not have any patients—"or they might come from all over the world."

Finch may have put on his best face and light touch, knowing that just two days earlier, convicted rapist Caryl Chessman had just barely escaped the gas chamber. Chessman's scheduled execution may have also played a part in Judge Evans sequestering jurors in a hotel as a precaution against them speaking with anyone outside the jury, an unusual but not unheard of move for a case that hadn't yet made it to deliberation.

*Grant Cooper, Finch's high-profile and
highly-paid criminal defense attorney.*

CHAPTER 36 – GRANT COOPER TIME

Finch's defense attorney Grant Cooper owed his career in law to a ship's broken steering gear. As a Bronx high school dropout, Cooper worked a series of odd jobs for five years when wanderlust hit. At age nineteen, he took a job as a wiper, the lowest rung on the oil tanker *Tulsagas*' crew. Twenty-three days later, he was in San Pedro, California. The ship was headed to the Orient, but Cooper decided he wasn't and jumped ship with eight dollars in his pocket. He wandered around the state and decided he might have been too hasty in making a decision. He gave being a seaman another try and signed up for a seven-and-half-day voyage to Eureka, near the Northern California border. Seasickness got the best of him, but it didn't stop him from signing up as a galley boy on yet another ship in San Francisco. But fate, as it has a habit of doing, intervened and when the steering gear broke after a day out at sea, the ship returned to port.

Figuring that the life of a landlocked attorney was much better than that of a seasick seaman, Cooper decided to take up his uncle John S. Cooper's offer to work in his law firm as a clerk and study law. He applied to Southwestern Law School in Los Angeles and was accepted, not only not having graduated from high school but without having a college degree. However, because of his lack of formal education, Cooper was required to maintain at least a 4.0 GPA, according to the *Los Angeles Times*. He graduated in 1926 and passed the bar exam the following year.

Cooper initially worked as a prosecutor in the Los Angeles District Attorney's Office and during his stint, served as a consultant on the 1946 MGM film version of *The Postman Always Rings Twice* with Lana Turner and John Garfield. The lack of significant financial rewards as a prosecutor and his experience positioned him to represent those on the other side of the law with immense wealth and indicted for crimes, like Bernard Finch. Cooper left the DA's office and soon struck out on his own and built a thriving law practice.

The San Gabriel Valley Tribune compared Cooper to John Wayne. At the time, there was no one outside of Dwight D. Eisenhower who could be used as the standard in the courtroom. Reporter Tom McCuaig went so far as to suggest that it was Cooper, not Finch or Carole, who was the star of the trial.

"The fatherly, gentlemanly, tremendously likeable lawyer...has won...the affections of the jury. [Jurors] smile when he smiles—which is often—and they pay close attention whenever he gets to his feet to make a point or record an objection.

"Cooper's performance has been superb and, win or lose, it must establish him as the Southland's greatest criminal attorney."

He may not have been the greatest but he certainly was in the top ten for going the distance—and beyond, which got him into trouble on behalf of his clients. Mobster Johnny Roselli and Maurice H. Friedman will later be accused of involvement in the 1969 Friars Club cheating card scandal in Beverly Hills. Cooper, who faced jail time, was fined a thousand dollars for contempt of court and publicly reprimanded by the state Supreme Court for illegally obtaining and using federal grand jury transcripts on Roselli's and Friedman's behalf. Cooper and his team lose the case and are accused of throwing it to avoid prison time in the Friars Club scandal. Prior to the Friars

Club case, Cooper had also represented Joan Bennett, and Shirley Temple in her divorce from actor John Agar. One future client would be Sirhan Sirhan, who will be tried for Senator Robert Kennedy's assassination in the nearby Ambassador Hotel ballroom kitchen. Sirhan is only spared the gas chamber when it is finally abolished in 1972 and his sentence commuted to life in prison.

Cooper's courtroom style included twirling or sucking on his glasses frames, and using his pipe to stand in for a murder weapon at the Finch trial. He disarmed and made prosecution witnesses comfortable on the witness stand, and once they were relaxed, went for the jugular. Smart and wily, he used every crack in the legal system he could find to his client's advantage and he would soon meet his match sitting in the jurist's chair during the second Finch trial.

To pay for Cooper's services, Finch transferred all of his property, including his home and ownership in the West Covina Medical Center and Labs, to Cooper. Among those transferred assets was Finch's beloved 1957 red Chrysler 300-C convertible, the automobile he sped around in many a drunken night, the car Barbara Finch drove the night she was murdered and figured so prominently in Finch's plan to kill her and what actually took place.

The 300-C was the fastest production car Detroit made when it began to roll off the Chrysler assembly line in December 1956. There was a standard 375 horsepower engine; a 390 horsepower engine was available as an option but not recommended for owners who had no lion-taming trainer experience or who stopped at red lights on their way to the local grocery store.

In addition to be being fully electrically powered, with its pushbutton automatic transmission and air conditioning, the car's tailfins, unlike those on other contemporary automobiles, served as stabilizers at high speeds. The 300-C was able to easily reach speeds of 130 mph. Air ducts below the headlights funneled cold air onto the brake drums to cool them. The car was even equipped with a windshield washer and 16 2/3 RPM record player, rare options at the time. Less than five hundred convertible 300-Cs were manufactured. Very few survive today.

Did Grant Cooper keep Finch's car after the trial to speed to the rescue of his clients? Or did he sell it?

Does the car even still exist?

Attention, 1957 Chrysler red convertible 300-C owners: time for a provenance check to find out if the infamous Dr. Bernard Finch "death car" is the one you own.

Or do you already know?

CHAPTER 37 – CLOSINGS

On February 22, a rumor made the rounds that a large amount of money had been made available to tamper with the jury, hoping the case would end in a mistrial. Whether defense attorneys were involved or not, none of them were accused in the alleged scheme. Instead, pundits looked to the Mob, which, as always, would benefit from bets being placed on the outcome. If the end result was a mistrial at a low price for organized crime, it would set a precedent for the Mob steering other high-profile cases to mistrial. Fortunately, Judge Evans was a step ahead and had already sequestered the jury, which had originally appeared to have been done to avoid any juror contamination from the upcoming Caryl Chessman execution. In sequestering the jury due to *any* potential tainting, Evans felt he also owed jurors an explanation—and a warning:

> You are all aware…of the widespread publicity this case has received, and…some pressure in and around us. You can tell the air is tense… I do believe it probably would be best to avoid the possibility of any embarrassment or any difficulty you might have [with] any individual who might decide to talk to you about the case. As you know, we have a good number of people traveling around the halls and otherwise with just such ideas.

The jury may have been sequestered, but it was also not on total lockdown in the Alexandria Hotel. To keep jurors busy and from sitting and stewing about their confinement, they were bussed together on weekend field trips. They visited Zuma Beach, the Santa Ynez Inn, Malibu Pier, the Ojai Valley Inn, and, much further east, the Mission Valley Inn. Just to make sure the bus wasn't followed or greeted at its destination by anyone who might interfere with the jury, jurors were not told beforehand where they were going. While ensconced daily in the hotel between trial sessions, they could leave their tenth-floor hotel rooms and go down to the third-floor banquet room, which had been set up for buffet meals, games, and television viewing. Jurors were allowed to watch bailiff-monitored variety shows, scripted programs, and movies on TV, but could not view broadcast news or discussion programs which might talk about the trial.

Still, all of this did not prevent bets being placed on the untampered outcome, including sub-bets for how long the jury would deliberate. There was one guaranteed winner: Jack Cody. Cody, who had not only been able to get out of his Minneapolis jail cell to go to Los Angeles to testify, was also paid for his services. He received five dollars a day ($43.77 in 2020) and ten cents (eight-seven cents in 2020) per mile, even though he didn't drive out for the trial. The mileage was a windfall for Cody since Minneapolis was 1,926 miles from Los Angeles.

Cha-ching!

The next day, the prosecution's summation began by "gravel-voiced" prosecutor Clifford Crail. He told the jury that Finch intended that two people die that night: his wife, Barbara Jean, and Marie Anne Lidholm (who then became an unintended witness to his plot to kill his wife). The real reason Finch returned to the garage after his wife died was to find Marie Anne. If she had been in the garage, Crail told the jury, he would have killed her too.

She has Mrs. Finch to thank [for her life]… if Mrs. Finch hadn't gotten out of that car and run down to her father-in-law's home, what do you think would have happened to Marie Anne?

Marie Anne told you that Dr. Finch did not call Carole at any time. No. he didn't call Carole. He knew where she was. She was waiting outside on the lawn with that little kit they brought to be called in at the proper time. Well, that time didn't come because of the resistance of Mrs. Finch and the intervention of Marie Anne.

Crail questioned Finch's wanting to administer aid to his wife in the garage after he had hit her. "Do you think they were headed for a hospital? If they were, wasn't that the time for Dr. Finch to say to Marie Anne, 'Call an ambulance and I'll try to keep Barbara comfortable'? Wouldn't you think that with his wife unconscious on the floor, if he had a hospital in mind, he would have called an ambulance? Since when is the proper treatment for a skull fracture to make a woman get off the floor and into an automobile?"

Crail moved to Don Williams' testimony, saying he "was torn between two desires; first not to injure Carole any more than he had to, and second, to tell the truth. When these desires came in conflict, I am afraid the truth suffered." And Carole once told Don Williams she "'would be quite happy when Mrs. Finch was out of the picture permanently.' I don't know how you could put her out of the picture more permanently than she has been."

Regarding Finch's and Carole's claim they hired Jack Cody as a detective: "If they were hiring a detective, why would they send him to Phoenix? If they were hiring a murderer to go to Los Angeles, they [might] send him by airplane to Phoenix so that he could take a bus to Los Angeles."

Crail told the jury how Finch weaved his story in and out of Marie Anne's because he knew the jury would believe her. The State believed that Barbara, unaware of what was going to happen, was hit by Finch when she exposed the left side of her head as she bent over to step out of the Chrysler. This was the only wound that produced much bleeding and, more importantly, the first skull fracture she received. This would account for the blood found in and on the left side of the car as well as why it was already there when Marie Anne entered the garage and saw the driver's door closed when Finch forced her into the backseat on the other side.

Crail finished his portion of the State's case, saying Carole was just as guilty as Finch, who pulled the trigger, because she conspired with him to murder Barbara. He questioned her story of hiding in the bougainvillea bush even after she heard a shot. *Why didn't she run out to see if Barbara had shot him?*

Because she knew Finch had the gun.

Why did she leave the attaché case on the front lawn? Did she forget it?

She left it because she didn't want to "risk being caught with it in her possession. The choice was hers. It was not something she overlooked." Crail finished with comparing Finch and Cody.

"Jack Cody's record is a series of arrests for drunkenness and disorderly conduct—I might say, somewhat of a fighting Irishman—who has had one conviction... Compare that with the string of things this fellow [pointing to Finch] said on the witness stand...of his personal life...of his deceptions... deceiving his bank, business associates...and then he comes in here and tells you Cody is not telling the truth, and *he* is?"

On February 25, Eddie Lindsey, twenty-eight, the sole African-American on the jury, had an impacted wisdom tooth and it halted the proceedings for the day, but not before Robert Neeb surprised the courtroom by hinting that Finch may have murdered Barbara, but Carole had no part in the conspiracy and was just an unwitting participant.

The next day, Jerry Giesler, who had been sick the past several months, recovering from a heart attack, arrived in court to watch his colleagues, Neeb, Bringgold, and then Eagan, sum up their defense for Carole. Neeb tried to distance Carole from Finch by saying she was not involved in a conspiracy to murder Mrs. Finch, nor did she do it—an innocent could accompany someone committing a crime and not be aware of it. This now presented a problem for Cooper in his defense of Finch.

After Eagan dismissed Carole from actually shooting Barbara, he took on the conspiracy theory, reciting the nursery rhyme "Three Men in a Tub." He referred to Cody, Keachie, and Williams as the "three men in a tub without an oar to get them to shore."

"Who gave them an oar?" he asked, then answered by pointing his finger in the direction of prosecutors Crail and Whichello. "They did. And what was that oar?

"Immunity from prosecution. Through that immunity, these two Minneapolis madonnas were granted carte blanche."

Carole may not have been crying but attorney Eagan was, as he painted prosecution witnesses Cody and Keachie in a bad light and Carole as virtuous when compared to them.

"Is it worth it to let Cody and Keachie walk the streets and kill this young girl?" He pointed to Carole. He also pointed out Carole's seeming ability to sit motionless, leaning on her left arm for long periods of time, as akin to hiding in the Finch home bushes for five or six hours without moving or being detected. Egan summed up the defense that, yes, Carole committed a crime—a crime of the heart falling in love with Finch. "If any blame attaches to Carole Tregoff, it is the age-old story of a girl in love with a man."

Visibly weeping, Eagan was finished summing up Carole's defense just as Dorothy Kilgallen predicted her team would.

But would the jury buy it?

Carole and one of her defense attorneys, Donald Bringgold. It was no accident her team sent a subtle message to jurors that Bringgold's and Carole's relationship might be something more than just attorney and client. The two played their roles convincingly. What juror would want to break Bringgold's heart by sending Carole to the gas chamber? The very-married Bringgold's wife might have disagreed.

On February 29, in a morning pre-session move in closed chambers, Grant Cooper tried to get Judge Evans to allow him to put a new witness on the stand: recently-unemployed *Times* reporter Conrad Staes. If allowed to testify, Staes would claim Marie Anne's testimony was questionable, that she could be persuaded to say anything by the police because he had been told as much by Detective Ray Hopkinson.

Evans denied his request. Instead, Grant Cooper made his case to the jury for Finch's innocence by saying the police jumped to the conclusion that Finch murdered his wife. He disparaged Marie Anne's testimony for a pattern of minor discrepancies, and claimed Barbara made wild accusations about beatings by Finch in order to cause him financial hardship in a divorce.

In a questionable move of first belittling, then asking for a favor, Cooper disparaged members of the jury. "It seems to me that one or two of you listen very closely to the prosecution, but while the defense is speaking, stare off into space." He then asked for their courtesy to listen to his closing. Apparently, vinegar worked better for him than sugar.

On March 2, Cooper finished making his closing statement for Finch. Finch, who had broken down and wept during Cooper's summation of Barbara's death, embraced and thanked him.

Whichello began the prosecution's closing argument on March 3 after a lunch break. The previous day, he dealt with Carole. Today, he related the 1937 case of Rattlesnake James who, with a friend, tried to murder his wife by sticking her foot in a box of rattlesnakes. Although she was bitten, the venom didn't kill her, so they drowned her in a bathtub and threw her body into a lily pond. Her death was initially ruled a drowning, but upon closer examination, it was discovered she had been bitten by a rattlesnake, thus convicting the two men of murder.

Whichello told the jury that although the original plan went awry, the men were convicted of first-degree murder based on their intent and premeditation, and that's how the Finch-Tregoff jury should consider this case. Neeb interrupted him and argued that Whichello's analogy was inflammatory and prejudicial, and called for a mistrial. Although Judge Evans agreed about the nature of the story and had it removed from the record and told the jury to disregard it, the rattlesnake was already out of the box. The story was not one the jury would likely forget—or that jurors would erase from their minds. Still, Evans did not call a mistrial.

Whichello talked about the defendants' hiring of Jack Cody to seduce Barbara. He told the jury that the defense was trying to insult its members. Could they believe that if Cody, a two-bit hustler and conman, was hired to seduce Barbara instead of kill her, would he not look out of place at the Los Angeles Tennis Club with a sophisticated woman like her?

"Hi ya, babe."

Even Finch described his wife as a lady and had to accuse her of frigidity to explain his affairs with the women at work. Maybe Barbara didn't like sharing her husband with the ladies of the medical center. Whichello called Finch a "monstrous liar" and the previous day had called Carole Tregoff a "latter-day Lady Macbeth" for urging Finch to plan the murder of his wife.

"She is really the aggressor and instigator of this whole thing" to kill Mrs. Finch. When Cody failed to do the job Carole and Finch hired him for, Carole prodded Finch into action.

Taking her cue at the defense table, Carole cried.

The next day, Whichello continued his summation for the prosecution by holding up what he told the jury was a major piece of incriminating evidence against Finch and Carole: a small, one-inch square empty envelope.

"This is the answer to your whole case, this little piece of paper. You recollect Mr. Neeb's little signposts that point the way to truth—well, here is an enormous signpost."

The envelope was inside a package containing a pair of sterilized surgical rubber gloves and had powder, which was to be applied to hands to make the gloves go on more easily. The fact the envelope was empty was telling, Whichello continued, for it proved Finch and Carole put on gloves to prevent leaving fingerprints at the scene of Barbara's murder.

The gloves were not used to play with Frosty, the family dog, and torn by him as the two claimed, but were used and disposed of by Finch and Carole in their execution of the crime. How could the dog get one of the fingertips from a glove and into the car where it was found? He couldn't. Whichello suggested that Finch and Carole were wearing them and lying in wait to carry out their plan to murder Barbara, and in the process of fighting in the car with Barbara, Finch lost the fingertip.

Whichello believed that as Barbara stepped out of the car, Finch hit her on the head and she bled on the car as she was momentarily knocked unconscious. She revived but bled on the garage floor and more on the car as she struggled with Finch. Barbara put up such a fight that Carole never got to play her intended role in the murder.

He took on Finch's dying-wife scenario and shredded it. Earlier, Cooper called Finch a consummate actor. Whichello responded, "I think he's a ham. He is even worse as a playwright and his performance was less than a class-B movie script. Can you conceive of that poor woman with a massive hemorrhage pouring into her lungs saying what he told us she said? Would she think it was accident? [No,] she would think it was *deliberate*."

He repeated Finch's quote of his wife's deathbed confession, "I should have listened."

"Listened to *what?* His *threats?*" A doctor would have administered first aid, which Finch didn't. Finch's fleeing the scene and stealing the cars were consistent with someone who had committed a crime.

Why would Barbara, a woman who had the advantage in her divorce filing, go along with Finch and move to Nevada to get a quickie divorce? Why did Finch and Carole come in the middle of the night to talk to her? A plan Barbara wasn't even aware of?

Finally, Whichello addressed the many tears of the defendants and their attorneys in court the past three months, clouding the very reason everyone was in court. "I wonder if it might be amiss if I said a word on behalf of Barbara Jean Finch. Somewhere in Southern California is a relatively new grave. In that grave lies the battered, broken, butchered body of Barbara Jean Finch, who, but for the activities of these two defendants, wouldn't be there. They can say anything they choose about Mrs. Finch and she can't rise out of the grave to give them the lie.

"Let us not forget about the woman they sent to her grave."

CHAPTER 38 – A SIMPLE CASE OF RACISM

The case was handed to the jury (five men, seven women) for deliberation. Crowds, hoping to get into the trial as spectators, did not disperse when deputies told them, at 4:30 p.m., the last closing had ended and the case had been handed off to the jury. Whichello, Cooper, Neeb, and Bringgold praised Judge Evans' decorum in guiding the trial, although that could not be said about the circus atmosphere outside. The attorneys also praised the press coverage as fair.

Unfortunately, California jurors were not allowed to have trial transcripts in their possession. Therefore, Cooper and Whichello had to read Finch's testimony to the jurors in court as Finch, Carole, and her attorneys looked on. Finch and Carole stared intently at his racehorse, Cooper, as he read his client's direct testimony beginning March 5. Whichello read the cross.

Finch's testimony continued to be read on March 7, first by Cooper, then Whichello. Cooper and Whichello continued alternately reading Finch's testimony on the following day. Finch and Carole stayed in a court anteroom instead of returning to county jail during jury deliberation per a defense motion. The readings were finally completed by 11 a.m. and the jury began its deliberations on March 9, which continued for the next three days. Jurors requested and were given a three-foot wide roll of grease paper to draw their own diagrams of the case while deliberating.

Unseen by the public, judge, and attorneys were insults, racial prejudice, and other antisocial behavior among jurors. Eddie Lindsey, the lone African-American, along with the only other minority juror, (Mr.) Dolores Jaimez, were both accused in separate news accounts of being the male juror who threatened fellow juror Genevieve Lang, saying "I'm going to pick you up and throw you out of the window."

Lang claimed the male juror (whomever it was, depending on the account) started to pick up the jury table then started to take off his coat, implying he meant to harm her. The male juror's actions caused one female juror to run for the buzzer to summon a bailiff and another to do the same by screaming and pounding on the door. It was later reported that the window couldn't be opened in the first place and, in one account, Eddie Lindsey apologized. Tempers flared because the jury had deadlocked three days earlier and no amount of arguing would convince anyone to change their mind or vote.

Foreman Lewis Werner would later say that Jaimez (who, according to a juror interviewed later, was mad that he was not selected as foreman and changed his vote from guilty to innocent) had influenced the black juror, Eddie Lindsey. Lindsey and Jaimez pledged unity to each other and kept to themselves.

Before the rancor broke out, Lindsey and Jaimez initially refused to free Carole Tregoff and give Finch a second-degree murder conviction. Juror Werner said that Jaimez and Lindsey believed the law was improperly written to recognize a degree of murder and because of such, they yelled, "Gas them or free them" at other jurors. Lindsey denied saying the law was improperly written.

"We voted our convictions," Jaimez said. "It is true that we changed our votes from guilty to innocent on the second ballot. But no ballot had been taken before the jury foreman was selected." Lindsey added, "The other jurors just didn't accept other peoples' views and argued irrationally."

The two minority jurors' votes to free Carole were joined by two of their white counterparts. Several of the women voted to convict her.

Finch was ultimately saved from a conviction due to racial prejudice against holdouts Lindsey and Jaimez. The racism was barely mentioned in Dorothy Kilgallen's column due to its general unspoken acceptance at the time.

"I know nothing of any racial prejudice," juror Beatrice Hindry later told reporters. "In fact, I lent Eddie Lindsey my manicure set at one time."

In the end, Stan Jacobson probably spoke for all the jurors when he said it "was a wonderful time to leave town for a week's vacation."

Other alleged events took place during deliberations: one juror made amorous advances via notes to three female jurors; one juror was sworn in under her theatrical, not legal, name and she was described as a "cultist" who believed God would take care of the whole thing, claiming that if Finch weren't punished in this world, he would be in the next. She eventually changed her vote to convict. Another juror later quipped, "Toward the end, she sure tried to help God."

On Saturday, March 12, after three days without a verdict, Judge Evans was at his home in Pasadena when he received word the jury had given the bailiff a note. It was deadlocked 10-2 for a Finch conviction; 4-8 for a Tregoff conviction; 4-8 for conspiracy. He headed downtown and called the attorneys and reporters into his chambers. "We are coming to the end of this thing and as long as we are together, I want to thank all of you of the press for your cooperation during the trial."

A reporter asked, "Is there anything to indicate how soon we are coming to the end, your Honor?"

Judge Evans replied, "No," then rose from his chair and moved around to the front of his desk. "Oh, I don't see why I shouldn't tell you. I'll make it short and sweet. The jury indicates they are deadlocked on all counts." Reporters couldn't get out of his chambers fast enough to get into phone booths. Judge Evans laughed and told those remaining, "I wish I could have told you that three weeks ago."

When Finch and Carole heard the verdicts, his face turned red and she cried. They knew they would have to live this nightmare all over again during a second trial.

Judge Evans dismissed the jury with instructions to them and reporters not to speak to one another. As jurors exited the courthouse, tired and wanting nothing more than to go home, juror Jaimez was spotted by Dorothy Kilgallen. Kilgallen had been flying back and forth from New York over weekends since the trial started in January for her appearances on *What's My Line?*

"Hello, I'd like to introduce myself. I'm Dorothy Kilgallen. You want to get home, don't you?"

"You're right," Jaimez responded. "All these questions." He waived over fellow juror Eddie Lindsey. The men followed Dorothy, who stepped off the sidewalk and into a clump of bushes, pulled them apart and revealed a taxi phone, which she picked up. Within a few minutes, they were whisked to the Ambassador Hotel, where Dorothy had been holed up during her Los Angeles sojourn, for drinks in her suite. They relaxed and talked about the trial, with Jaimez producing a jury journal he'd kept, while she documented what the two men told her. She got on the phone to her paper and asked for someone who could take quotes from the men over the phone.

What she may not have told them in her hotel room was that an article of hers published in papers (including the *Orlando Sentinel* on March 11 with news likely from the 10th) hinted that the trial was likely going to end in a hung jury due to a juror holding out. What she did not say in print was that she knew the juror's identity.

Was it Jaimez or Lindsey?

Did she purposely target Jaimez on the sidewalk as he exited the courthouse knowing he was a holdout?

Somehow, Kilgallen had gotten someone to leak information on the jury's deliberations to her. That, combined with her befriending local newsstand seller Eddie Bright, who tipped her off to the hidden taxi phone, which gave her not only a jump on the other reporters—but her exclusive with Jaimez and Lindsey.

The question at the time—and still to this day—was whether Finch and Carole knew they were spared, at least momentarily, from prison—possibly even the gas chamber—due to racism.

Or were they just too full of themselves to consider what had happened among jurors and how close they came to being convicted?

The next evening, actor William Talman, who played Los Angeles District Attorney Hamilton Burger on CBS' *Perry Mason,* happened to drop by for a drink at friend's home in Hollywood. He was soon arrested by police, along with seven other men and women, for participating in a nude marijuana orgy where the partiers were found in various stages of undress. None of the eight, however, were prosecuted on a narcotics charge.

"How can a person have marijuana in his possession when he didn't have a strip of clothes on his body?" asked Deputy District Attorney John W. Loucks. Apparently, body cavities were out of the question. Actress Lola De Witt, one of the eight arrested, was asked about the nudity.

"Well, we were comfortable. We were having a sociable gathering. We were a compatible group, very friendly. In our business people have to relax, you know."

Relaxed or not, Talman protested his innocence but was still fired by CBS. But just nine months later after the marijuana embers and the public's memory had died down, Talman returned almost midway through the following season with the support of producer Gail Patrick Jackson and star Raymond Burr. Talman's personal life didn't end so happily. The previous August, his wife Barbara divorced him over his "late hours."

"When I asked my husband where he had been after he came home late, he would tell me it was none of my business," she told Judge Elmer Doyle.

The next day, after Talman was arrested, real-life Los Angeles district attorney, William McKesson, possibly recalling the actor's pot-infused saturnalia the previous night, vowed that the second Finch-Tregoff trial would not devolve into something less becoming a courtroom trial under his watch.

"There will be no more circus court and no more hippodroming," he promised reporters, scheduling the second trial back in one of the smaller Hall of Justice courtrooms to contain it from disreputable outside—and inside—forces.

As McKesson would soon find out, the size of the "container" didn't matter when the principals in it were crazy actors from the start.

242 | STEVE KOSAREFF

PART III

CHAPTER 39 – SECOND TRIAL PRELIMINARIES

On March 14, District Attorney McKesson announced that the prosecutors from the first trial, Whichello and Crail, might not work on the subsequent second trial, even though earlier, Whichello said he would.

The next day, Robert Neeb moved to have Carole released on bail since, among other things, he believed there wasn't a high probability of conviction at the end of the trial for his client. There was indeed fact for Neeb to base this on. Although most jurors voted to convict Finch, most voted to acquit Carole. In doing so, they may have recalled Rex Eagan's plea for mercy at the end of his closing.

Don't kill this beautiful, young woman.

In addition to the racism on the jury panel, a reverse case of sexism may have saved her from *any* degree of conviction.

To head the defense off at the pass, McKesson announced he would strongly oppose bail for both Carole and Finch.

Grant Cooper decried McKesson's announced investigation into potential juror impropriety regarding physical threats and sexual harassment. McKesson avoided dealing with the real reason the jury deadlocked. Did he not see the racism? Or did he just want to dodge a powder keg the majority-white culture at the time was all too happy to step around?

Cooper pooh-poohed McKesson's investigation. "I am personally convinced that any investigation that may be made will do no more than point up the fact that sharp differences of opinion and personality clashes are not unusual among jurors in any case where there can be an honest difference of opinion." Cooper said nothing about racism among the jurors or the fact it saved his client from a potential death sentence.

Robert Neeb also needled McKesson about his jury investigation. "Just because the case went against the prosecution is no reason to call for an investigation. Would McKesson want an investigation if he had won?"

McKesson, in his absence, had acting DA Manly J. Bower set the wheels in motion for his investigation by inviting jurors to attend a meeting with him and Judge Evans.

On March 17, Judge John G. Barnes set May 23 as the date for the second trial to begin, denying Neeb's request for a separate trial for Carole. He granted Carole twenty-five thousand dollar bail, but denied bail at any cost to Finch. The following day, Carole was released and headed home with her parents.

The next day, Gladys told the press Carole wanted to shed the twenty-seven pounds she had gained on a prison diet so she could fit into her dresses. James prepared a hamburger-and-onion dish for dinner. So much for the diet. Instead of counting calories, Carole relaxed in a bubble bath before dinner and refused to speak to the press or take phone calls. The *Herald-Express* saw a great opportunity for a headline the following day:

"Finch's Mistress Takes Bubble Bath, Eats Hamburger."

On April 6, Judge LeRoy Dawson was named to preside over the retrial, set for May 23, joining previously announced Deputy DA Joseph Powers (who replaced Whichello) and returning second prosecutor Deputy DA Clifford Crail, who, although his team didn't get convictions, his prosecution style was impressive.

Now thirteen pounds lighter, on April 14, Carole, in a beige wool dress with matching gloves, purse and shoes, and Finch appeared at a pre-trial hearing with their attorneys. When she was led into the courtroom in handcuffs and spotted Finch, she reportedly silently mouthed, "I love you." When he was led away back to jail, she sobbed. But she soon got another chance to see him. Still out on bail on May 4, she tagged along with an associate from Grant Cooper's law firm, who was delivering a message to Finch and visited him in jail.

The May 23 start date for the second trial passed without court convening. On June 9, Robert Neeb discussed the possibility of using Carole as a witness against Finch in hope of having charges against her dismissed. Did she visit Finch in jail to get information she could use against him or did she plan on telling him what her attorneys were up to and asked for his blessing? It soon didn't matter. Within a week, after reading an article wherein DA McKesson stated, "They're just wasting their time if all they want is a dismissal," Neeb changed his mind and canceled the appointment with the DA's office.

If Carole and Neeb had met with McKesson what might they have told him?

That she and Finch didn't go to talk to Barbara about a divorce?

That it was a murder conspiracy from the start that she engineered but later regretted?

That the attaché case was intended as a murder kit?

That Finch was going to neutralize and kill Barbara and put her body in the Chrysler?

That Finch was a vicious killer in a doctor's smock?

That she didn't hide in the Bougainvillea bush but ran directly to her car?

The possibilities and combinations were mind-boggling.

Carole's team attempted to remove Judge Dawson from presiding over the trial for "prejudice" through the California Supreme Court (which rejected it) and the US Supreme Court (where the petition awaited review but was denied two days later).

Finally, on June 27, a month after it was originally scheduled, the second Finch-Tregoff trial began back where it originally started, in the Hall of Justice, with the first prospective jurors being interviewed. The question remained why Carole's attorneys tried to have Judge Dawson removed from the trial even before it began. What worried them so much about Dawson that they tried to unseat him with Jerry Giesler getting out of his sick bed to make a case before the state Supreme Court? Did they know—or find out— about Dawson's high conviction rate and multiple death sentences? Had one of Carole's attorneys represented a client in Dawson's court who was convicted of murder and sentenced to death? Or was it because Dawson didn't suffer fools gladly and was known for being thorough?

Did the thought ever occur to Carole's team that in its attempt to remove Dawson, it might produce the same result as poking a stick at a venomous snake, which might be worse than letting him preside over the trial?

Whatever the attorneys thought they were trying to prevent by having Dawson removed must have been far worse than what they could have possibly imagined might result from their attempt. In either event, Dawson's removal didn't matter to Rex Eagan anymore. Three days after the trial began, he quit, citing poor health, and Dawson excused him from serving as part of Carole's team. Was the timing of Eagan's withdrawal from the trial and Dawson's appointment a coincidence? Or did Eagan just not have the stomach to defend Carole in a Dawson courtroom?

"I'm going home to rest, in the hope that I can stay out of the hospital," he told reporters about his abdominal ailment.

If Eagan had gone to a physician, would the doctor have prescribed two Alka-Seltzer for a case of Dawsonitis? Whether Eagan's stomach pains were real or imagined, Donald Bringgold was now on his own as Carole's attorney. Although Robert Neeb and Jerry Giesler represented Carole as partners in Giesler's law firm, they would now only act as counsel and not share Bringgold's courtroom duties.

On July 11, Carole broke down and sobbed during a courtroom recess, leading some to speculate there was a rift between her and Finch. Three days later, I broke down and sobbed at my grandparents' home in Granada Hills when I was told by my grandmother that my mother had just given birth to her third girl in a row.

I cried because I wanted a brother. Now I would be outnumbered in my family, three to one by girls, that even being the oldest child and a boy could never trump. The lone male Finch-Tregoff juror knew what I was crying about when the next day jury selection was completed and he realized he was also outnumbered, but by eleven women. This fact did not go unrecognized by several of them, who sized up their fellow jurors and sought out the weakest among them. Three of the women decide to target the lone man. They later bullied him during jury deliberations, brought him to tears, and were called on the carpet for it by Dawson.

Several days after the birth of my new sister, Diane Gail, I was picked up from my grandparents' house and driven home to Covina with all three sisters and my thirteen-year-old aunt, Shirley, to help my mother while she recovered from her C-Section. I arrived and faced the second bonechilling surprise of the week: my tabby kitten, Puff, who mysteriously appeared in our yard several months earlier, had now mysteriously disappeared. My mother explained that he had run away from home since there was no one around to feed him while she was in the hospital and my father was working. Even at the age of eight, I knew that a pet, who was loved and fed, would not run away. Her story sounded fishy and I brought it up over the years, especially every time I viewed home movies of him.

It took almost forty years before my mother finally admitted the truth about Puff's disappearance: he was taken to the local dog pound. How does a parent separate their child from a beloved animal? I can only chalk it up to my mother's own childhood when she was torn away from the people she loved and shuttled between relatives like an orphan. The lack of permanence and connection was imprinted on her at an early age and that's why she had no second thoughts about throwing out my personal belongings after I moved away from home—and even the cat before I left.

My mother's mistake was not getting rid of the evidence of Puff's existence; in this case, the home movies with him. Every criminal knows to destroy photographs or film footage of their crime, including the *Perry Mason* character who sent his wife in their car over a ravine and was caught doing it on home movies.

Of course, it could be argued that when my mother shot the footage of Puff, she had no thought at the time to make him disappear. Even still, I love and miss my mother, who passed away in 2012 . But the bereavement I felt as an eight-year-old who lost his kitten sixty years ago has never gone away.

It never will.

Carole requires some assistance to appear in court
on the one-year anniversary of Barbara's death.

CHAPTER 40 –
CALLING IN SICK

Carole knew July 18, 1960, was the one year anniversary of Barbara's death and the beginning of her living nightmare. The thought of going through a second trial made for one too many bad dreams for her to stomach. She called in sick with hives the next day by sending a friend, Joyce Earnhart, to tell her attorney, who, in turn, reported her absence to the court. Judge Dawson was furious that the young woman had defied the court. He sent the jury home and ordered jail physician Dr. Marcus Crahan to the Tregoff home to check out Carole's hives.

Dr. Crahan arrived with a female deputy, Gabrielle Johnston, and after taking Carole's temperature, pulse, and blood pressure and finding them normal and no hives on Carole's face, reported back that she was fine. Crahan and Johnston were told to bring her to court. But Carole had another idea. Deputy Johnston fought to dress her as she refused to cooperate. Carole slapped Johnston in the face and kicked her in the stomach when she wouldn't let her go into the bathroom alone. There was a stand-off and deputy re-enforcements were called in to help. Dawson ordered her bail revoked and put out a bench warrant for her arrest.

Several deputies were now dressing Carole, and with her outnumbered, they finally succeeded. Johnston handcuffed Carole and the other deputies dragged her, kicking and fighting, out of the Tregoff home to a station wagon waiting at the curb. She was taken to the county jail and removed from the car against her will to be processed. She was caught by a photographer as she was pulled from the station wagon in her lessthanusual celebrity-flattering state.

Instead of her glamorous, celebrity arrival at the West Covina courthouse a year earlier in sunglasses and mink-collared suit, Carole now arrived at the Hall of Justice courtroom in an unkempt state, hair mussed, no makeup, and wearing the old blue housedress she was put in by deputies. But somehow, she still managed to have an intoxicating effect on Finch, who, like everyone else in court, had been waiting for her arrival. Finch dabbed her tears and offered another handkerchief, fawning over her like a child who stubbed her toe. It was all too much for Judge Dawson.

He took umbrage with Finch's overly attentive concern for Carole in her present state and warned him, "There is entirely too much solicitude being shown in this courtroom." Dawson also refused to reinstate Carole's bail due to her behavior.

Was she throwing in the towel by calling in sick and not cooperating with judicial procedure? A contemporary *Herald-Express* reporter described her post-arrest mood as a "sleepwalker attitude." A psychologist spectator called Carole's state of mind "almost catatonic."

During the court proceedings, she buried her face in her arms on the counsel table or stared blankly into space as a storm cloud of attorneys hung over her head, arguing heatedly over the next few days about her bail and how she should be referred to when court was in session. Her stepmother told reporters that "she acts like she belongs in the psycho ward."

Paging Frances Farmer!

The next day, Judge Dawson told the courtroom that alternate juror selection would continue. Bringgold interrupted by trying to get Carole released on bail and told Dawson that he had proof of Carole's illness the previous day.

"We will be hearing nothing today, Mr. Bringgold," Dawson warned him.

Bringgold protested, "But, Your Honor, I have Dr. Garnett here to testify."

"Mr. Bringgold, we are not going to hear from anybody today on anything but this jury."

"Your Honor, this concerns the health of my client."

"Mr. Bringgold, *sit down!* Please."

The following day, the four alternates were chosen. Bringgold continued to fight for Carole's bail, but Dawson was unmoved. Arguments continued among counsel on how to refer to Carole. Bringgold's referral to her as "Carole" or "the girl" was thought by prosecutors as a bald-faced attempt to engender sympathy. Judge Dawson settled the question by saying she should be referred to as "Miss Tregoff" or "the defendant."

On July 22, Jack Cody was arrested for grand larceny in St. Paul, Minnesota. He was given the option of going to jail or going to Los Angeles to testify in the second trial. He chose the latter, recalling his good fortune when he was paid to perform his one-man show and basked in the courtroom spotlight. Did Cody orchestrate his arrest once he found out about the second trial to take another paid vacation to Los Angeles at taxpayers' expense?

Finally, her personal drama over, Carole settled into the swing of things in the courtroom. She was in a better mood. She took notes and wore her hair in a truncated ponytail—not the glamour-girl bouffant in West Covina—but a step up from her disheveled appearance a few days earlier.

CHAPTER 41 – THE HOUSE
ON THE HILL, PART II

On July 25, just as the first jury did, the second made a field trip to Lark Hill Drive. It was very warm on the hilltop in West Covina, but not as hot as it was three days earlier when the temperature bordered on one hundred degrees. Judge Dawson called court to order at 10:40 a.m. with the jury in front of the Finch garage while Carole and Finch, as they did on their previous visit, with their backs to the court, admired the view of the San Gabriel Valley from the driveway. Unlike the winter visit, the warm, summer-induced smog created a haze that blocked most of their view across the Eastern San Gabriel Valley up to the mountains. If the blanket of smog suggested a curtain slowly coming down on their play, they pushed the thought aside and nervously joked with each other as a dry, warm breeze blew through Carole's once-again auburn hair.

Unlike its appearance in January, the Finch property had been revitalized. Plants were alive, the grass green, the trash-filled puddle in the pool gone, the pool cleaned and filled with freshly chlorinated water—all because the home had been sold and was now occupied by a new family. Owner W.C. Dearth (who moved in earlier in the month) paid fifty thousand dollars for the property, a bargain basement price in exchange for moving into a home where someone had recently been murdered and the owner was forced into a fire sale. Apparently, the Dearths, whose last name was one letter shy of what occurred on the property the previous year, weren't superstitious or afraid of ghosts. But there was one thing they couldn't avoid: Barbara's death on the premises and the resulting public fascination with the crime, which drew unwanted tourists to the property. There was nothing like an unnatural death in a home that has a life beyond the people who reside within. Sixty years later, the home is still a magnet for crime buffs.

There was an upside. Mr. Dearth didn't have to pay someone to stand in line for him to see the show now gathering outside his front door. He walked out a few yards to view the courtroom proceedings on his driveway.

After Judge Dawson and the jurors moved down the driveway to Finch's parents' home, his sister Marian Gordon came out to speak to him. Finch had been denied permission to see his invalid mother inside the house. But he had an idea. As jurors moved around to the other side of the property, he yelled out to his sister, "The den!" and shortly thereafter, a window opened and a woman in a wheelchair appeared.

"Hi, Mom."

"Hello, son."

It was the first time Bernard Finch had seen his mother since the previous jury's visitation of the property in January.

CHAPTER 42 – THE
SECOND TRIAL

Unlike the first trial, prosecutors decided to have witnesses appear in chronological order of events to keep things straight in jurors' minds. Once the jury returned to the courtroom after the field trip to Finch's home and lunch, Marie Anne recounted her testimony from the first trial.

Grant Cooper had trouble over the next few days with witnesses who remembered more details regarding Barbara than they shared at the first trial. Are witnesses' memories sharper upon reflection over the past several months? Or are they more creative? A memory of a memory is a second memory and not necessarily the truth. Cooper put this axiom to test on June 27. When he cross-examined Barbara's divorce attorney, Joseph Forno, he questioned Forno's ability to remember a statement he made at this trial about Barbara, but not at the first one.

"I have remembered it since she made the statement," Forno answered.

"You didn't testify to that in the first trial." The prosecution objected and Cooper continued, "Well, I can read his whole testimony if counsel wants."

Judge Dawson snapped, "Maybe you can, but you won't!"

"Your Honor, I have the right to examine someone on the rules of evidence," Cooper responded.

Dawson was firm and final. "If an objection is sustained, that's all there is to going to try this case on the evidence at this trial, not at the other trial."

Cooper did catch Forno in a mistake from the first trial in the transcript when he claimed Barbara was beaten twice by Finch, on May 18 and then again on June 25, but Forno now said it was once.

Minnette Haber, Don Williams, and Jimmy Pappa testified again and repeated what they said at the first trial. After Jimmy left the stand, he and Carole made eye contact and exchanged hellos.

Jack Cody also testified. On August 1, he admitted he had lied for money. Cody was taken to task by Cooper, who read his testimony from the first trial, which infuriated Judge Dawson. The judge didn't want the jury misled by testimony from the earlier trial. Cooper accused the judge of judicial misconduct, claiming he was not misleading the jury, to which the judge clarified what he meant and if he said "misled," to have it stricken from the record. He wanted the jury to focus on what witnesses said at this trial and testimony from the first trial should only be used on an impeachment or an attempt-to-impeach basis.

Cooper wanted to ask Cody if he'd gotten any favorable treatment for his testimony, but Judge Dawson disallowed it, with Crail voicing his disgust that any deal had been made. Before the lunch break, Dawson instructed the jury to disregard conversations between the court and the attorneys.

Carole was fashionably dressed with a new hairdo, low-cut, full skirted, blue print dress, pink sweater, and her famous red high heels. She spoke with Finch during a bench break.

The next day, Donald Bringgold took his crack at Cody on behalf of Carole. He tried to pin Cody down on his inebriation the night he discussed doing a job for Finch with his associate, Richard Keachie. "Was it possible you were drunk when you had the discussion?" Bringgold asked.

"There's always a possibility I might be drunk," Cody responded, "but I don't remember being drunk." Cody referred to this stage of his inebriation as "half stiff."

"Half stiff? What does that mean? How does that affect your memory?" Bringgold asked.

"When I'm half stiff, my memory is just as good as when I'm sober," Cody replied.

Cooper and Dawson continued to clash. During Cody's testimony, Cooper accused Judge Dawson a third time of judicial misconduct when Dawson allowed Cody's testimony from the first trial, but stated as he did, "Well, I don't think it's important, but we'll do it."

Navy Commander John Behr (whose fiancé, now wife, Betty Jean testified in the first trial) testified about their dinner with Barbara the last night of her life. "Did you observe a .38-caliber Smith & Wesson in that bag?" Deputy DA Joseph Powers asked in regards to Barbara's purse at dinner, disputing Finch and Carole's claims that she pulled a gun on them.

"No, sir," Behr replied.

The jury was temporarily dismissed when Crail claimed Cooper had spoken to prosecution witness Keachie in his office, who had in mind to change his testimony and receive compensation. Cooper admitted to Keachie's visit to his office, but no deal was made. He claimed Keachie told him he was offered a deal similar to Cody's for his testimony by Fred Whichello.

Crail questioned Cody about the leniency Cooper claimed the state would provide in exchange for his testimony. Cody was testifying not out of getting leniency, but out of fear of being charged with a more serious crime: conspiracy to commit murder. He'd be happy to serve the two years for a less serious crime he was convicted of in Minnesota. Cody, upset, by the exchange, offered to take a lie detector test.

The next day, Cody was back on the stand again. He was asked by Cooper about how he was going to fare with Minnesota authorities for his crimes in the state. "I could get the maximum—two years—and be happy up there. I could wake up every morning with a smile on my face. My worry has been California and a conspiracy charge," Cody explained.

"Conspiracy to what?" Cooper asked.

"Conspiracy to murder."

"With these defendants?"

"Yes," Cody replied.

Crail was on his feet, objecting, which Dawson sustained and then asked Cooper where he was leading. Powers accused Cooper of bad faith. Cooper appealed wordlessly to Dawson by throwing up his hands. Dawson looked over him at the jury. "I say to this jury now, I don't think you're acting in bad faith."

Crail jumped in, "At this time."

"Your Honor!" Cooper pleaded.

"Yes," Dawson responded. "The words 'at this time' will be stricken."

Cody was confronted with a character witness, Dan Prila, who was present at the time in a Hollywood bar when Cody appeared to tell a Jack Whalen he would soon have the money he owed him from a doctor who hired him to follow his wife.

"I never saw him before in my life," Cody responded. Prila laughed.

On August 8, Marie Anne was back in the hot seat. Cooper went after her in his cross. He claimed that all of her previous accounts of the night of Barbara's death—to the police, at the hearing, and the previous trial—weren't the same. The stress was too much for her and she broke down and cried, "I don't remember everything I said that night."

The next day, Crail explained the differences in Marie Anne's testimonies via her changing skills with the English language from her native Swedish. Crail explained that at times she was saying yes, not as an affirmative response to a question but as a polite response to confirm she was listening. Cooper objected that Crail couldn't legally go into those statements on a redirect examination. Crail accused Cooper of saying the witness was making up things. Cooper explained that he didn't think Marie Anne was lying, that he considered her an honest witness, but thought that she was mistaken. Crail'd had enough.

"Mr. Cooper, you have said that you want to be fair to this witness. Now you attempt to prevent me from showing that she has made consistent statements in the past."

"Don't shout," Cooper responded.

"I'm not shouting but you burn me up when you make statements like that."

"No use burning up in here," Judge Dawson interjected. He upheld Cooper's statement that he had not accused Marie Anne of fabrication and his objection to the line of questioning.

Taking all this in was thirteen-year-old Patti Dee Daugherty, Barbara's daughter who lived with the Finches. When it was her turn up to bat, Patti told the little she knew, hearing her mother's and Finch's loud voices in the garage, a "banging around," and her mother's scream for Marie Anne to come to her assistance. She waited in the house for Marie Anne's return and upon it, stayed with her while Marie Anne called the police. Cooper wisely did not cross-examine her.

On August 10, West Covina Police Officer Donald Rund testified about discovering Barbara's body in bright moonlight. She had been shot once in the back. Officer Meehan identified the murder kit and its contents, which he claimed he received from Finch's father. Again, how did Meehan view the contents of the case without the key to open it, which Detective Hopkinson was given by Las Vegas sheriffs?

Did Hopkinson give Meehan the key after Raymond Finch gave him the attaché case? Did Meehan even open the case? This was never explained.

Was it possible they did it together?

Was one of them lying?

There was a new witness at the trial that was not at the first. Finch's neighbor, Georgina May, told the court that a floodlight, usually on in evenings, was not on the night of Barbara's death, suggesting her death was pre-meditated and not an accidental shooting. Detective Hopkinson testified he found a stick near the floodlight that may have been used to disconnect the electrical cord from its outlet.

On August 11, Donald Williams took the stand again, this time as a defense witness, claiming he did not receive a car from Finch for his services as Cody claimed he had and, under cross by Crail, said he knew nothing about a murder or illegal plot by Carole and Finch against Barbara.

Detective William Ryan was cross-examined by Cooper regarding his notes with Marie Anne the night of Barbara's death. Ryan explained that she was speaking fast, was upset, and spoke in an accent he had trouble understanding. Cooper pointed out his note about her hearing "shots," which she had testified she heard one in the garage and the other as she was entering the home to call the police. Ryan said he wrote the notation later, but to his best recollection, "shots" was what she said.

On August 15, coroner Gerald Ridge testified that although Barbara's gunshot wound would hamper her ability to speak after about forty or fifty seconds, there could have been a "transitory clearing of consciousness" during the throes of death and therefore he couldn't confirm her inability to speak. Sheriff's chemist Clifford Cromp testified that another type of pistol was used to test for the shooting distance, but with a second test, a gun more like the one used in Barbara's death was fired from one to two feet.

On August 17, Cooper accused Judge Dawson of judicial misconduct for a fourth time when he sustained a prosecution objection.

On August 18, Ridge testified about the alcohol level in Barbara's blood at the time of death.

On August 19, what would have been Barbara Finch's thirty-seventh birthday, Carl Mossberg testified about his station wagon being stolen the night of Barbara's death. Officer Booth testified to finding Mossberg's car in the driveway of his home. Also testifying was Leon Surruys about his stolen red-and-white 1955 Cadillac, which Finch used on a high-speed chase with police on the San Bernardino Freeway and to escape to Las Vegas. Even with Surruys having used the car, police found no prints on it. Not his, not Finch's, not anybody's, including gas station attendants.

How likely was the car not to have any human prints?

It is doubtful prosecutors asked Surruys about the capabilities of the Cadillac and its condition the night it was stolen. If they had, they might have been able to take apart Finch's claim that he was in not in a conscious state from the time right after Barbara's death to his arrival in Las Vegas.

Was the car's fuel tank full the night Finch stole it?

The car's gas tank could hold up to twenty gallons of gasoline and Cadillacs manufactured the same year averaged somewhere between 10-13 MPG on the highway. If the gas tank to Surruys' car was full when Finch stole it, he could have made it to Las Vegas without stopping for gas. If it wasn't full—even slightly—Finch would have had to stop for gas.

If so, how out of it could Finch have been if he was still able to wipe his fingerprints off the car, and stop and ask a station attendant for gas? Was he still wearing the latex gloves he had on when he murdered Barbara to prevent leaving fingerprints? Or did he pick up an extra pair when he stopped at West Covina Hospital?

Detective Ryan also testified about Carole making a statement in Las Vegas that she had seen the murder kit in the back seat of her car the night she drove with Finch to West Covina, but that she hadn't touched it, and of her later testimony at the Finch hearing that she carried the murder kit up to the Finch house.

On August 22, Judge Albert Miller testified again about Carole's behavior in his court during the Finch hearing. Gubser and Powell, who found Finch and Carole sleeping in her apartment at different times and picked them up for questioning, also testified.

On August 23, as Donald Bringgold cross examined Gubser, he questioned whether it was standard practice to get a key from a landlord to enter an apartment. Before Gubser could answer, Judge Dawson told him it was, to which Cooper objected. Cooper and Dawson went another round when he requested that the judge's answer be stricken from the record.

On August 24, Carole and Bringgold suffered a major blow: Judge Dawson ruled that testimony Carole gave at the Finch hearing (Exhibit 60) was admissible: her affair with Finch, what she saw and heard the night of Barbara's death, and the attaché case. The next day, her entire transcript from the Finch hearing was read to the jury as she watched in horror.

On August 29, Cooper made his three-hour opening statement for Finch, then Bringgold gave a one-sentence opening statement. "We expect the evidence to prove the innocence of Miss Carole Tregoff" and called her to the stand.

CHAPTER 43 – WHAT DID YOU DO IN THE APARTMENT?

The next day, August 30, Bringgold continued with his questioning of Carole, including how she believed that Jack Cody was a detective. Then, under heated cross-examination by Crail, Carole was forced to say what went on between her and Finch in their rented apartment.

"Why did you rent the first Monterey Park apartment?" Crail asked.

"So Dr. Finch and I could be together," she replied.

"What did you want to do?"

"Well, anything we wanted to."

"*What did you want to do?*"

"We had lunch occasionally… we listened to records. We talked."

"What else?"

Carole began sobbing and buried her face in her hands. Dawson called a fifteen-minute recess. When she returned, composed, she answered the question in almost a whisper, "We made love." Crail continued his course, asking her why she said "no" at the hearing when asked if she and Finch had been intimate.

"'No' was an exclamation, not an answer," she responded.

Later, when asked if she perjured herself at the Finch hearing, Cooper, who was not her defense attorney, jumped up and objected. Judge Dawson ordered him to sit down after Crail pointed out Cooper was not her attorney. Cooper did, but not before saying the judge was unfair. Dawson ordered the jury excused and then proceeded to take umbrage with Cooper about his being "unfair."

"I'm not having any lawyer stand up and tell me what to do or how to run my court. I'm not being unfair and I'm not having you or any other lawyer tell me I am, in front of a jury and a crowded courtroom," Dawson tore into Cooper.

After an agreement that none of Carole's testimony would have any bearing on Finch, Cooper apologized, and after Dawson ruled that Cooper could object whenever he wanted, the jury was called back in.

The next day, August 31, Deputy DA Crail hammered away at Carole about discrepancies in her statements to police and the first trial regarding the murder kit. He grilled her about speaking to Finch in Las Vegas after their return from West Covina, just before he was arrested, concocting the story she was telling now, and the payment to Cody. The next day, Crail grilled Carole for the third and last day.

"He was the biggest thing in your life?" Crail asked.

"At that particular moment," she responded.

Crail attacked. "Oh, do you have moments when he's the biggest thing in your life and moments when he isn't?"

She did not respond.

Crail produced an enlarged photo of Barbara, dead, in front of Carole. "What do you see on Mrs. Finch's face?"

"I can't tell."

"You see blood, don't you?"

"Yes, sir," she whispered.

Crail presented Carole with her contradicting testimony that she had never been around guns and he pointed to the earlier trial testimony that she had shot at sharks with Finch off Catalina.

A "graying and pallid" Finch, due to a year in jail, detailed to Cooper on September 2 how he made money on top of money at West Covina Medical Center. Deputy DA Joseph Powers was so disgusted he objected, telling the court he didn't have to listen to Finch's Horatio Alger story. "We aren't interested in the mechanics of how he acquired his fortune."

Judge Dawson overruled him and allowed it, but cautioned Cooper to limit his background on Finch. Four days later, Finch's statement to Las Vegas sheriffs after he was arrested and told about Barbara's murder was read by Cooper to the jury, including his response to his statement to sheriffs about the murder.

"It sounds like a cheap melodrama that you read in a dime novel."

Finch began to describe the night of his wife's death as an accident. At the defense table, Carole leaned over in her low-cut dress to speak to Bringgold. Finch frowned, stopped testifying, and got her attention. He pulled his coat lapels closer together, signaling to Carole to assume a more modest appearance. She smiled at him, then realized the top of her dress may be exposing more than she planned, or what Finch thought was proper at a murder trial. She blushed and pulled the collars up, more in deference to Finch than modesty since pinning would be the only way to keep the dress from falling back to its designed focal point.

Finch was questioned by Cooper about a conversation he had with Cody ten days before Barbara's death. Deputy DA Powers objected to Finch's answers and Cooper asked Finch if he could remember the exact words, to which Finch replied, "No, I cannot, but I can make some up if I have to."

"That's the most truthful thing he's said," Crail said privately to Powers, but loud enough for Cooper to overhear and claim misconduct.

"He was only discussing the case with me," Deputy DA Powers interjected. "We can't help it if Mr. Cooper is listening in on our conversation."

Judge Dawson had not heard Crail's crack. Cooper told the court he was sure some of the jurors heard it and repeated it. "Well, now that everybody's heard, the jury is instructed to disregard it," Dawson settled the matter. Without the emotion of the previous trial, Finch relayed the death of his wife for the court on September 8, in front of Cooper, which, instead of creating tears in jurors as it did in the first trial, caused some of them to snicker and try to contain their laughter. When Cooper demonstrated with his pipe how the fatal shot may have killed Barbara, spectators were later admonished to stop laughing with a threat to clear the courtroom by Judge Dawson.

Four days later, Powers made a list of Finch's legal violations on a blackboard: assaulting his wife, assaulting Marie Anne, theft of two cars, possession of narcotics and hypodermic needles in Nevada, reconciliation pact perjury, and adultery. Finch admitted to Powers he had no legal right as a doctor to carry narcotics in Nevada.

On September 14, Cooper accused Powers of degrading and embarrassing Finch by yelling at and referring to him as "Mr. Finch." On September 16, Powers continued to keep Finch focused, asking for yes or no answers.

"Did you pull the trigger that fired the bullet into your wife's back?"

"Obviously I did" Finch replied, but still claimed the shooting was an accident.

Powers questioned Finch's return to the garage after his wife was shot. "Didn't you consider Marie Anne a piece of unfinished business?"

"No!" Finch shouted half standing up. "No, no, no—I didn't go back there to do anything to Marie Anne!"

On September 20, Raymond Finch, Bernie's father, brought Barbara's wedding and engagement rings into court at the request of both the defense and prosecution. The jury members passed the rings around to get a closer look. The rings had been retrieved by Raymond from a silverware case in her and Bernie's home and now resided in a special boxed setting created by Raymond to display them in the best possible light.

He took the stand as a witness and was asked if he was awakened the night of the shooting. He said he was, about 12:15 a.m., but did not mention that he thought, or hoped, it was due to a car backfiring. Raymond did not exit the house to investigate the noise. The police came to his home.

"When you were awakened, did you know there was a body on your lawn?" Crail asked.

Raymond said he did not. What did the police say to him? Were they just checking to make sure he and his wife were all right? Why did Raymond not pursue the police? Was it to avoid the inevitable and keep the wolves from the door just a little bit longer?

On September 23, Dewayne Wolfer from the LAPD crime laboratory was a rebuttal witness to Finch's claim the gun accidentally went off when he threw it, killing Barbara. Wolfer said when the type of gun Finch used was cocked, it only took a three to four pound pull to fire it. When the hammer was not cocked, it would take nine to thirteen pounds to fire.

"Are there any features that make it impossible to fire this gun without the trigger pull when it is cocked?" asked Powers.

Wolfer demonstrated two safety factors and said his lab tested a similar gun with blanks and threw it against a concrete wall. It did not discharge.

Finch had just been accused of cocking the gun that "accidentally" killed Barbara.

On October 4, Powers finished his closing and Bringgold started his. He ended the next day with tears in his eyes and a shaky voice. "Carole Tregoff, I turn your destiny over to God and this jury."

On October 20, the deliberations for the second trial were handed to the jury.

The next day, Carole got the number two dishwasher job in jail to avoid being alone with her thoughts. Dr. Finch took part in choral hymns during church services in jail. "He's a good baritone," one of the jailers informed.

What the two of them didn't know was that a week later on October 27, the jury sent word to Judge Dawson. It had agreed on a verdict of second-degree murder against Finch and deadlocked on Carole.

Dawson turned it down.

Why?

CHAPTER 44 – JUDGE LEROY DAWSON AT YOUR SERVICE

On November 3, the jury questioned Judge Dawson regarding punishment for the various degrees of murder conviction. "What is the punishment for first-degree murder, second-degree murder, and conspiracy—and is there time off for good behavior?"

Dawson responded, "You have been instructed that penalty is not to be discussed at this proceeding. I will say…that this is a case where you should be able to reach a verdict." The jury filed out and Grant Cooper rose.

"Your Honor, the defendant Finch takes exception to Your Honor's preemptory instruction to the jury…in which Your Honor said that this is a case in which they should be able to agree."

Judge Dawson retorted, "He can take all the exception he wants to. It is a fact I believe. And I think I have a right to say so."

"I respectfully request Your Honor to instruct the jury to disregard your remark."

"I will not!" Dawson barked, ending the discussion.

The next day, with the jury seemingly deadlocked, Judge Dawson had prepared a statement and read it to the jury in an attempt to get it to make a decision. He extraordinarily stated:

- The jury should believe Jack Cody;

- Finch and Carole lied about their reason for driving to West Covina; and

- Finch's story about shooting Barbara was not an accident.

Cooper strenuously objected to Dawson's statement and was cited twice for contempt. "Dr. Finch went white and his jaw dropped. Carole paled and her attorney Donald R. Bringgold [was] starte[l]d, as if unable to believe his ears," reported the *Herald-Express*.

Finch and Carole wept in court, their bodies heaving with sobs as they listened to Dawson's statement to the jury. He told jurors he was not trying to sway them to make a decision one way or the other, but he had a legal right to comment on the evidence. Those in "the minority ought to seriously ask themselves if they were justified in continuing to oppose the views of those in the majority.

"If you determine that the defendants are not telling the truth regarding the purpose of their visit to the Finch residence…then they must have a reason for not telling the truth, which would be, of course, that the truth would not establish their innocence, but, on the contrary, would indicate their guilt."

Grant Cooper jumped to his feet, but Dawson's radar had already locked on him.

"Now, Mr. Cooper, I don't want a word out of either of you counsels, and I instruct you and Mr. Bringgold to be seated. You are not going to argue in the presence of this jury."

"But, Your Honor, you are invading the province of the jury—"

"Mr. Cooper, I hold you directly in contempt of this Court!"

"That's Your Honor's prerogative."

"It certainly is, and I'm going to exercise it."

Dawson instructed the jury not to consider Cooper's contempt citations during deliberations and Cooper jumped up again.

"Just a minute. You sit down," Dawson warned Cooper again. The bailiff ran over to try and calm Cooper but he continued to protest, bringing another warning from Dawson. "I hold you in contempt, Mr. Cooper. You have no right to say anything in the presence of this jury."

The jury began filing out, but Cooper would not be silenced.

"I do have a right to object... I still feel I have a right. Never in the history of the Courts of California have I seen such an occasion in which the Court invaded the province of the jury."

"That may well be," Dawson responded, "but when I told you not to say anything or argue in the presence of the jury, you shouldn't do it, and when I say 'sit down' that ends it. The only thing I could do was hold you in contempt. I still have the responsibility for this Court."

"At all times, I have respect for the Court but I do not intend to apologize. I was only doing what I thought was right in representing my client, and I'm ready for sentence."

"I don't want an apology. But you don't have the right to continue to express an opinion contrary to the opinion the Court is expressing in the presence of the jury."

And back and forth it went, until Cooper suddenly called for a mistrial, with Donald Bringgold joining him. Clifford Crail, however, had the last word. Bringgold had just previously referred to Cooper's status as president of the Los Angeles Bar.

"As long as Mr. Cooper is president of the Bar, he should act it," Crail retorted, essentially ending the war of words.

In addition to Dawson's right to make a statement to the jury, Dawson may have also wanted to pay back the defense attorneys for the multiple times they tried to have him removed for prejudice from the trial even before it began. A few days later, Dawson told reporters that he bent over backwards giving Cooper a lot of leeway regarding contempt during the trial to not appear prejudiced. Did the defense inadvertently cause what it was trying to prevent by attempting to remove Judge Dawson? It appeared so.

On November 7, 1960, the jury was hung 9-3 for first-degree murder and conspiracy for Finch; 9-3 for first-degree murder and conspiracy for Carole. The three holdouts found Jack Cody unbelievable. Juror Lillie Nielsen, who believed him, reported "personality conflicts, anger and tears" prevented the jury from coming to a unanimous decision. "The nine were subjected to insults by the three. Personal insults and otherwise," she stated. "When you make a man cry, you have to be insulting," she stated referring to bullying Foreman Edwin Fry.

Judge Dawson let loose with his anger and not only castigated Grant Cooper for his behavior during the trial, but also the three female jurors for not following their oath as he saw it, even being lesser women for doing it. Dawson's wrath did not stop there. He also called out Foreman Fry for not being man enough to stand up to the three women, a very public emasculation if ever there was one.

Disgusted by everyone, Dawson declared a mistrial and scheduled a third trial start date for January 3, 1961. Finch and Carole accepted the mistrial declaration stoically. They knew the drill, having been through it before. The defense filed a motion for double jeopardy, claiming the jury did find Finch guilty of second-degree murder and acquitted Carole. The Sheriff's Department was looking into the charge, along with two alleged improprieties by female jurors, including being too friendly with James Tregoff, Carole's father.

Just as the defense attorneys' attempt to remove Dawson early on backfired, Dawson's remarks to the jury that he believed the defendants were guilty may have backfired on him. "They seemed to make us more firm in our convictions and they angered the holdouts. The whole thing seemed to make them more stubborn—if that was possible," juror Fru Tooraen told the *Herald-Express*.

On November 24, Marie Anne managed to evade being served a subpoena to testify in the third trial and made her way home to Sweden. The *Los Angeles Times* reported that the first two trials cost taxpayers one hundred and seventy-five thousand dollars ($1.5 Million in 2020).

The first trial lasted ninety-five days and the jury deliberated for thirty-seven hours.

The second trial lasted one hundred and thirty-three days and the jury deliberated for seventy-one hours.

The second trial was supposed to be streamlined.

This was not a good omen for the third trial.

CHAPTER 45 – THE HOUSE ON THE HILL, PART III

On January 23, 1961, the third trial jury visited the scene of the crime in West Covina. It was the third visit for a group of jurors to the property. Raymond Finch asked the court if his son might visit with his mother. Third-trial judge David Coleman denied it, saying it wouldn't be fair to do so in front of the jury.

But that didn't stop the Finch family.

Finch purposely lagged behind the group as it toured the property and his sister, Jane Wagner, came out of the family home and from the front porch waved at him and yelled, "She's at the window!"

Finch walked as close to the open window as he could to see his wheelchair-bound mother on the other side. "Hi, Mom."

"Hello, Bernard."

"Can you see me all right?" he asked.

"Yes, yes, you're looking fine," she responded.

"I wrote you a letter," he told her.

"Yes, I received it," she replied.

Finch smiled and said, "See you later," turned, and walked off, waving to her as he rejoined the group.

CHAPTER 46 – THE
THIRD TRIAL

Previous to the jury's visit to the Finch properties, juror selection began on January 3, presided over by Judge Coleman. On January 16, nine men and three women were picked. Maxwell Keith, an associate of Grant Cooper, had taken over Finch's defense due to Cooper's upcoming surgery and prior commitments.

Six days later, Marie Anne returned from Sweden of her own volition and cost courtesy of the Superior Court to testify. The next day, testimonies began. They moved twice as fast as the previous trials, as exhausted attorneys raced for a finish line—any finish line. Clifford Crail and Joseph Powers had returned for the prosecution, as had Donald Bringgold for Carole Tregoff. The setting was in an even smaller courtroom in the old Hall of Justice that seated only eighty spectators, many seats going unoccupied, the public also obviously tired of a rerun of *Perry Mason* for the second time.

Lidholm, Jimmy Pappa, and Joseph Forno testified. There was a much different attitude between Jimmy and Carole than at the second trial. They saw each other briefly and shared a private joke during a recess before he took the stand. They exchanged smiles—with Finch even smiling at him—although whether Jimmy returned it or snarled at him was not recorded. Jimmy took the stand to tell his version of Carole's torrid, home-wrecking love affair with Finch, bookended by his and Carole's lovebird behavior in the courtroom. When attorneys approached the bench, Jimmy and Carole smiled at each other and she covered her mouth to keep from laughing out loud.

On January 25, Jack Cody testified for a third time about the payment by the defendants. The next day, he told the court that after he informed Carole he had shotgunned Barbara, she merrily responded, "Oh, I'm so thrilled!"

He suggested to Carole that Finch let Barbara have the money and he and Carole relocate to another town and start their lives over. But Finch still wanted to go through with the plan and told him, "It has to be done."

"Are you sure you want to go through with it?" he asked Carole, "Because once I get on that airplane, you can't call me back," He told the court she assured him she wanted to.

The next day, under cross by Bringgold, Cody told the court, in his opinion, he's a man who kept his mouth shut. A paradox after all his chatterbox testimony. "I think I told her I'd been in this kind of thing my whole life," he informed Bringgold.

"What thing?"

"Keeping my mouth shut," responded Cody.

On January 30, Cody testified that Finch wanted to kill him for failing to deliver the murder-for-hire. Not stated in the first two trials, he told Bringgold why he left Las Vegas.

"I heard Finch was looking…to kill me." Almost in the same breath, he told Bringgold that he could have been testifying for the other side if only Finch had come up with some money for his defense. "I'd be right with them, on their side in this, today."

CHAPTER 47 – THE HOUSE ON THE HILL, PART IV

Unlike the first two juries, something about Finch's story about how his wife died didn't make sense to the third. Jurors requested a second trip to the Finch properties and it was granted. On March 9, they went back—the only jury to do so. This time, jurors paid particular attention to the garage. Judge Coleman told the jury they were not to speak to one another or discuss what they were viewing.

Finch, now pale from the lack of sunlight and stress, shed tears. Carole had gained back the weight she lost while out on bail and wore the same loose-fitting blue-and-white plaid dress as in the first trial, with only lipstick for makeup. Without the fashion access afforded her by bail, she also had a major run in her left stocking. Finch was free of handcuffs, but at one point when the deputy who guarded him thought he was lagging behind the group, yanked him by the arm. It was a not-too-silent reminder of the reason he was able to visit his once prized home.

Nonetheless, having a handler didn't stop him from doing a jig and acting like he was going to jump or dive in when the group was near the empty swimming pool, which drew a broad smile from Carole. During the tour of the home and grounds, they talked to each other, but stopped when anyone else approached. Once again, they stayed in the yard of his former home when the jury silently moved to his father's yard where Barbara died.

The next day, March 10, prosecutor Joseph Powers began his summation. Following would be Maxwell Keith, who had taken over from Grant Cooper, Donald Bringgold, and then Clifford Crail.

Maxwell Keith was a thirty-six year old graduate of Princeton and Loyola Law School, with greying disheveled wavy hair. His courtroom style said he had read *To Kill a Mockingbird* one too many times since its publication the previous July. He channeled Atticus Finch with a wacky, humorous bent, intentional or not, on the floor of the courtroom. Keith began his closing argument for the real-life Finch.

"Ladies and gentlemen, I am awed at being here, and by my great responsibility. I don't feel well-endowed to carry it because Mr. Powers has sent a lot of people to the gas chamber. I don't have any experience like that. I have never even tried a murder case. But I am going to do my best.

"Dr. Finch is not insane."

A few days later, Keith, coatless, drew Judge Coleman's ire when he rifled through the evidence box and pulled out Finch's recognizable murder night togs, the red plaid shirt, and alpine hat. Keith put them on and stated, "What a murder outfit!" in mock disbelief, in an effort to devalue their importance. Spectators and jurors alike laughed, to which the Judge Coleman drew umbrage.

"What do you think is funny about this, ladies and gentlemen? Anyone who thinks it funny will leave the courtroom… Put your coat on, Mr. Keith," he reprimanded the defense attorney like an errant school boy who had been caught acting up by making the kids laugh in the classroom behind the teacher's back.

"Yes, Your Honor," Keith sheepishly drawled as he removed the shirt and hat.

Nine and half years later, in December 1970, Keith would be appointed to represent Leslie Van Houten and Patricia Krenwinkel, two of Charles Manson's notorious girls, and Charles "Tex" Watson, all three tried for the Tate-La Bianca murders in August 1969. The attorney Keith replaced representing Van Houten was Ronald Hughes, whose body was found in a creek near his campsite a few months later. No signs of foul play were ever discovered, but the timing appeared to be too much of a coincidence for those who loved to speculate about untimely, high-profile deaths.

Keith was determined to represent Van Houten and *not* Charles Manson. Whether Manson had Hughes killed or not, Keith must have occasionally looked back over his shoulder.

CHAPTER 48 – THE VERDICT

March 23, 1961

The case was placed in the jury's hands. During Crail's summation, juror Elizabeth A. Stevens dramatically collapsed in the jury box for a second time in a week and was replaced by an alternate, Arthur E. Reed, a retired builder. The jury now comprised of ten men and two women, which from past experience would appear to work in Carole's favor.

It was noted in a newspaper article that Finch took reams of notes during the third trial, and there was some speculation he may appeal his case from jail if he was convicted, similarly to convicted rapist Caryl Chessman. Prosecutors told the press that if the third trial resulted in a hung jury, they were prepared to move forward with a fourth trial—something which had never occurred in California.

March 27, 1961

4:15 p.m.

The foreman sent Judge Coleman a note. The jury had a question: was a conspiracy charge a conflict if one conviction was for first-degree murder and the other for second-degree? The judge sent back, "My answer is no. There is no conflict." Reporters ran to payphones as the courtroom stirred, knowing a verdict was likely imminent due to the judge's note.

5:15 p.m.

Three staccato bursts from the buzzer in the jury room. The jury soon delivered its verdicts: Finch was guilty of first-degree murder, and Carole of second-degree murder. Both were found guilty of conspiracy to commit murder. Both could face the death penalty; she because of her conspiracy conviction.

"My God, after all this time!" Finch exclaimed to the courtroom.

Judge Coleman ordered the jury to return the following week for sentence deliberation, and the convicted to be returned to jail. Finch moved over to Carole and put his arm around her, saying "I love you, Carole... I'm sorry" but what followed next was a matter of contention.

The Los Angeles Times reported, "Still sobbing, she sank into his arms, burying her head in his shoulder"—the gist of which the *Herald- Express* also supported, while the *San Gabriel Valley Tribune* reported "she twisted away from him and was helped out of court by jail matrons."

What may have actually happened, according to another printed account, was a combination of the two: when Finch reached out "he forced Carole into an embrace—and then suddenly, tears streaming down her face, she withdrew coldly and walked out of the courtroom without saying a word." She ignored her attorney, Donald Bringgold, while Finch's, Maxwell Keith, apologized to him. "I'm sorry, real sorry." Finch interrupted and patted him on the back.

"It's alright, Max."

The three trials were estimated to have cost three hundred thousand dollars (almost $2.6 million in 2020).

Reporters spoke to Jimmy Pappa and Marie Anne Lidholm. Pappa was sorry they were convicted. He didn't believe that Barbara's death was deliberate. He didn't think it was a good idea to see Carole, but would take her back.

Twenty-one-year-old Marie Anne seemed to have the more considered take. "I'm sure glad we finally got a conviction. But I don't believe in capital punishment. I hope there is no death penalty. I don't believe one person should take another person's life, even if it's by law. We're not capable enough to judge another when it comes to taking a life. Carole was old enough to know what she was getting into. I really do feel sorry for Carole. I always felt she wasn't as guilty as Dr. Finch. But since they conspired, they should have the same penalty. Carole always cried during the trials. Now she really has something to cry about."

Over the next few days, Carole refused to eat while Finch ate spottily and slept with a blanket pulled over his head. She did speak to her father for about fifteen minutes the following day in the visitor's area. While Carole refused to eat, jurors, who would at long last be released, dined their last night together on "pineapple scrub, molded fruit salad, thick-cut New York steaks, baked potatoes, Italian-style spinach, and fresh strawberry shortcake." After dinner, they said their goodbyes and piled into three station wagons to be driven home. They would return to court on Monday to begin the penalty phase deliberations.

Speaking from New Orleans a few days later, where he was attending an attorneys' conference, Grant Cooper told reporters that the jury may have been cowed by the prosecution into its guilty verdict. Members may have felt they would be persecuted if they sided with the defense based on the DA making an investigation into jurors who voted not guilty in the first trial, and the judge, who publicly castigated jurors in court who voted against conviction in the second. Crail took umbrage with Cooper long distance and called his statements "an obvious effort to influence the jury" in a violation of court rules. Crail said a case against Cooper was pending the outcome of jury's penalty determination.

Finch and Carole finally recovered from their initial shock. He played chess with fellow prisoners and she resumed her jail food server duties, but the penalties for their crimes had to be weighing heavily on their minds.

Would they die in the gas chamber?

CHAPTER 49 – THE PENALTY

April 3, 1961

Penalty Hearing

Both Carole and Finch showed signs of stress as they entered and sat down at counsel tables. The outside temperature reflected the emotion in the courtroom, hovering around ninety-three degrees. Los Angeles County was posed to call a smog alert. The only thing missing was a wild fire in the local mountains.

Maxwell Keith made an impassioned plea: "If you order Dr. Finch executed, you and I and everybody here will be with him in the gas chamber when they drop those gas pellets" Likewise, Crail, last to speak after Powers, Keith and Bringgold, made one for the death penalty, telling the jury it was being asked to "show a mercy toward these defendants they did not show Barbara Jean Finch." Crail brought an end to the penalty summations. Penalty deliberations were then handed off to the jury.

Finch walked over to Carole at the counsel table. "Carole… Sorry… I love you."

"Goodbye. No matter what happens, I love you," she told Finch in what might be her last words to him, especially if either received the death penalty.

Popular Los Angeles Western swing musician and television host Spade Cooley was arrested that evening for murdering his wife. The coroner reported she either died from a ruptured aorta due to blows to the stomach, or being choked, rupturing the thyroid. Cooley admitted to "slapping her around a bit." Finch likely heard about the Cooley murder that evening from his cellmates or a jailer. The stress of his own murder conviction and pending penalty combined with the report of Cooley's murder might have coalesced in Finch's sleep that night by their starring together in his long-delayed nightmare.

Were the two men waiting for Finch's alter ego at the end of a conveyor belt?

While the jury debated Finch's and Carole's fates, the news in the papers the next day about Cooley must have been seen as a bad omen for the defendants and their attorneys.

April 5, 1961
3:24 p.m.

The jury buzzer rang. Jurors filed back into the courtroom, as did Finch and Carole, who had been waiting all day in an anteroom. The jury had a question and it was read in court.

"Is it possible to return a verdict of life imprisonment with the possibility of parole?"

"No," Judge Coleman informed the jurors, who left to deliberate once more. Carole and Finch were ushered back to an anteroom to wait.

4:15 p.m.

The jury buzzer rang three times. The jury filed in, along with Carole and Finch. After deliberating twelve hours, they had a verdict: life terms for both Finch and Carole.

Grant Cooper, scared when he saw the expressions on jurors' faces, was happy with a life sentence for Finch. Finch, paunchy and haggard from two years in jail and three trials, knew he narrowly escaped the death penalty and breathed a major sigh of relief.

"Thank God, thank God," he muttered. He reached out to touch Carole, whose head was bowed as she wept. "Don't cry, we'll fight it, darling. We're still alive."

"No, no, no. I'll be an old woman when I get out," Carole moaned upon realizing she may have escaped the gas pellets, but now faced the rest of her life behind bars.

Finch and Carole were convicted when the jury, after visiting his home a second time, reenacted the murder with juror Mildred R. Brown playing the part of Barbara, she told reporters. This act occurred after attorneys had closed, but before the jury began its deliberations. The jury realized through its recreation of the struggle between Barbara and Finch that Finch was lying about how his wife was shot. The jury did not believe Finch's story of the struggle with Barbara over the gun in the garage, nor that Carole stayed hidden in the bushes. The jury also did not believe the timing of Finch's and Carole's hazy memories about the night of Barbara's death. The jury did believe Marie Anne's testimony and, most critically, Jack Cody's that he was hired to kill, not seduce, Barbara.

Carole was convicted of conspiracy because she hired Jack Cody and because she carried the murder kit from her car up the hill to the Finch home. She escaped a first-degree murder conviction because she did not handle the gun used to murder Barbara.

Finch and Carole's downfall pivoted on their hiring a confidence man instead of a professional killer to murder Barbara. Carole worked at the Sands Hotel, which was then owned and operated by the Mob. Didn't it occur to Finch and Carole that she should try to get an employee at the Sands, who was connected, to hook them up with a paid assassin? Or were they just too cheap to pay the going price? Why didn't Finch forge the check for a larger amount? Or did he fear Barbara—or the bank—would notice? Finch and Carole's decision to hire a bargain-basement "killer" was ultimately their undoing.

Due to California law, Finch and Carole would be eligible for parole in 1968, even though they would be serving concurrent life terms for murder and conspiracy.

After all that had occurred—Barbara's murder, Finch's loss of his estate, nearly two years in jail and now facing lifetimes in prison—were the pair were still in love?

Donald Bringgold responded, "Undoubtedly. They're very much in love."

CHAPTER 50 – THE AFTERMATH

April 20, 1961
Finch was taken to Chino men's prison, and Carole to California Institute for Women at Frontera, near Corona.

April 25, 1961
The Finch home sale netted $16,675 after the mortgage was paid. Funds were split three ways, with thirds each going to Raymond Jr., Patti Dee Daugherty, and Grant Cooper for legal fees.

June 6, 1961
Finch was transferred to San Quentin. Upon his arrival, he told the associate warden, Dale Frady, that he wanted to marry Carole when he was released.

August 7, 1961
Four months after the last trial ended, Los Angeles television station KHJ aired the 1953 film *Angel Face* every night for a week as part of its Million Dollar Movie program. In the film, Jean Simmons planned on killing her stepmother by tampering with the car she was driving, forcing it to go over a cliff on the family's hillside home. Unfortunately, and unknown to Simmons' character, her father hitched a ride with his wife and she accidentally killed him as well as intentionally murdering her stepmother. Did the station program the film based on its similarity to the planned murder involved in the last Finch-Tregoff trial? Jean Simmons – Murderess With an Angel Face!

October 1961: Jerry Giesler suffered another heart attack, this time the most serious one. He did not fully recover and passed away on January 1, 1962.

May 4, 1964: Finch, who had converted to Catholicism two years earlier, was a prison tennis champion and a model prisoner.

July 6, 1964: Finch's medical license was finally revoked almost five years after Barbara's murder.

May 1, 1969: Carole Ann Tregoff was paroled from prison and picked up by her parents.

October 29, 1971: Dr. Bernard Finch was paroled after serving ten years of a life sentence. Lean and fit, he ran ten miles a day and played tennis. Prior to his release he had been out on three seventy-two-hour passes to seek employment. Upon his release, Finch was given a party at Charlie Brown's restaurant in West Covina, attended by family, friends, and prison guards. Notably absent was Carole Tregoff under her new moniker.

But Finch was not without female company at his welcome home party. He was accompanied by a young brown-haired woman in her early thirties known as "Miss Davis." Although she was about the same age and bore a striking resemblance to Carole Tregoff, a prison spokesperson said Miss Davis could not have been Miss Tregoff "because the terms of his parole specifically prohibit his association with any former felons."

Picked up from prison by his father and an unidentified woman (later identified as "Neva Davis"), Finch ignored the thirty-five reporters waiting for him outside the gates. He hopped in the driver's seat of his father's car and sped out of the facility at 8:25 a.m., wearing a baseball cap and sunglasses, with Neva by his side and his father in the back seat.

Was Finch able to get a driver's license in advance of his prison release? If not, was he taking a chance on being arrested for driving without one after just having been released from prison? If the latter, it would have been interesting to see what would have happened if Bernard Finch was pulled over by a police officer in a similar fashion to his old days of drunken driving.

Finch initially stayed with Raymond at his home just across from the scene of his biggest hopes and dreams and worst nightmare. Bernie's mother and Raymond's wife, Marian Eva, had passed away seven years earlier in 1964 after years of poor health. If Finch's years in prison weren't enough punishment, his time staying with his father in his parents' home without his mother's presence surely was not how he planned on greeting the world upon his release.

Oh, how far Dr. Bernard Finch had fallen from the time he was King of the San Gabriel Valley.

December 3, 1971: After a two-year campaign and a delegation's visit to him in prison to secure his employment in El Dorado Springs, Missouri, the town's civic leaders hired Finch as an x-ray technician until he could get his medical license back. Now with his hair longer in an early 1970s style, the town welcomed the former doctor. Unfortunately for Bernie, the pesky Neva, who had maintained a correspondence with Finch in prison and then began to visit him, had also driven east with him. He contended that their relationship was nothing more than a friendship, and might jeopardize his securing a medical license.

"This type of thing just seems to follow me around. I told her I can't afford to see her," he understatedly replied. Nor did he seem to have learned a lesson about his past with women.

September 24, 1973: Overriding the ruling of the Missouri State Board of Registration, the Missouri State

Administrative Hearing Commission was ordered to allow Finch to take the medical exam for a license.

May 23, 1974: Finch somehow finally managed to rid himself of groupie Neva and married Elizabeth Kehoe, fifty, a psychiatric social worker he met in prison.

June 1975: I was sick with a case of strep throat and a friend drove me from my Santa Monica apartment to West Covina Medical Center. I was treated by Finch's former brother-in-law, Dr. Franklin Gordon, who had been my family's doctor for over twenty-five years now. Dr. Gordon and I had not seen each other for almost ten years, since before I graduated from high school.

I told Dr. Gordon I was living near the beach in Santa Monica and he said the clean air there was better for my respiratory issues than the smoggy San Gabriel Valley. We did not speak of his brother-in-law. He treated me for the strep and I was driven back by my friend to Santa Monica to recover. It was the sickest I have ever been in my life to date.

I never saw Dr. Gordon again. He passed away in 2011 at age ninety-six; his wife, Finch's sister, Marian Louise followed two years later, age ninety-three. How had they managed to survive the personal and professional setbacks that Brother Bernie caused them all those years ago?

June 1977: Bernard Finch, still without a medical license, was running a medical clinic in Bolivar, Missouri.

January 28, 1984: After his return to California, the State finally reinstated Finch's medical license. He practiced medicine in Rancho Mirage near Palm Springs, where he loved to play tennis, and close to the Salton Sea, where Carole once loved to water ski behind his boat.

To this day, the gun Bernard Finch used to kill his wife Barbara has never been found.

CHAPTER 51 – THE NON-SMOKING GUN SCENARIO

July 19, 1959

Uninjured on the run, Bernie still drove his second stolen car to nearby West Covina Medical Clinic and Hospital. He parked the car in the mostly-empty lot and grabbed something from the seat, jumped out of the car, half closed the door, and ran into the hospital through a delivery entrance. He made sure to avoid areas where an overnight doctor or nurse on duty might see him, and made his way to a hazardous waste disposal receptacle.

He opened Barbara's purse. He pulled out the gun, the bullet, and the shell casing, and threw them into the can, making sure they fell to the bottom where they were unlikely to be found. He next threw Barbara's purse in and also made sure it fell to the bottom. He looked around to see that there were no witnesses to his disposal of the murder evidence and, with no one in the vicinity, ran out of the building the way he came in. Bernie jumped in the red-and-white Cadillac he had stolen, started it, and exited the parking lot toward the Orange Avenue entrance.

As he pulled the car out of the parking lot, he was spotted by patrol officers, who were looking for him. Dr. Bernard Finch jumped on the San Bernardino Freeway and headed west towards Los Angeles with the officers in hot pursuit.

He would soon be on his way back to Las Vegas and, hopefully, Carole.

AFTERWORD

January 14, 2020

Dr. Raymond Bernard Finch passed away in 1995 at age seventy-seven from natural causes and was buried in the family cemetery at Oakdale Memorial Park in Glendora.

I believed that Barbara Finch remained buried at Oakdale where she was interred on July 24, 1959. Then my companion, Paul L'Esperance, surfing the internet, found a post for her burial site at Forest Lawn Covina Hills, some six miles away. It appeared that the family had Barbara disinterred and moved to put some distance between her and the Finch family once Forest Lawn opened in 1964. This appeared to me to be even more likely if she had been buried in a Finch family plot. Barbara's exhumation could have occurred after Dr. Finch's burial in 1995.

But something still didn't feel right.

I decided to get to the truth and made a trip to Forest Lawn the Sunday before the above date to locate Barbara's gravesite. Even working with two receptionists searching the Forest Lawn database, I still came up empty handed. There was a Barbara Jean Reynolds (her maiden name) buried at Forest Lawn, but the birth and death dates didn't match. I decided to go back to where I knew Barbara had been buried at one time. I called Oakdale and left a message; my phone call was returned about ten minutes later. Yes, a Barbara Jean Finch, who died on June 18, 1959, was buried at Oakdale.

Now my detective wheels were spinning. I had to find the gravesite. The following Tuesday, I drove to Oakdale and was given a map and directions to the burial site, but even with the map, I couldn't find the grave. I went back to the office and an assistant drove me back to the area in a golf cart. We searched but had no better luck. She called her office and asked for the names of the people buried on either side of Barbara. Armed with the names, we searched and finally found the gravesite. To my surprise we discovered that Barbara Jean Finch's gravesite was… unmarked.

But why?

Was it possible a family member decided to purposely misdirect researchers like myself to Forest Lawn to keep us away from Oakdale? The assistant, without knowing Barbara's story, offered that maybe it had slipped the family's collective mind to follow up and purchase a headstone. But I knew the more likely reason: the family decided to keep the public away by not identifying Barbara's gravesite with a marker and give her what she was denied in life. Peace.

After returning with the assistant to the reception building, I decided to find Dr. Finch's gravesite again. I drove over to the area where his grandfather, Thomas Finch, was buried. I knew the site was located near the Gordon Family Mausoleum, next to a flagpole. Finding Thomas Finch and his wife Malisa's headstone, I crossed the roadway and worked my way up to where I remembered his grandson's location.

Finding Dr. Finch's headstone, I looked up in the direction of Barbara's gravesite and, lo and behold, to my surprise, it was within sight. I walked back to her unmarked grave and counted the rows and distance from Barbara's to Dr. Finch's: four rows behind her and approximately one hundred yards to the left. Against her likely wishes, Barbara had, in a way, been reunited with Bernie. It was the proverbial nail in her coffin.

Try as she might to stop the domestic abuse she suffered at the hands of her husband—calling police, seeking comfort by telling friends, hiring a divorce attorney, hiding a crowbar

under her bed, running down the driveway to get away—
ever since her husband's burial in 1995, Barbara Jean Finch,
even in death, would never escape the man who murdered
her.

ACKNOWLEDGMENTS

This book would not exist without the support of WildBlue Press and its founders, Steve Jackson and Michael Cordova. Gentlemen, thank you for taking a chance on a first-time true crime author. I also want to thank those in the trenches: Publishing Director Ashley Kaesemeyer, and Social Media and Public Relations Manager Natalie DeYoung. Ladies, hope I wasn't too much of a pain.

Even though a significant portion of this book is based on my experiences and memories of being a patient and member of a family treated by Dr. Finch, the bulk of the story would not exist without significant research. I am grateful to those who helped me in that endeavor. I want to thank the librarians of the Los Angeles County Library at West Covina, California, and the main branch of the Los Angeles City Public Library for their help in accessing newspaper archives on microfilm. I would also like to thank the Los Angeles County District Attorney's Office, District Attorney Jackie Lacey and Special Assistant Cheryl Gaines for locating the transcripts for the Bernard Finch-Carole Tregoff trials and making them available for my review. I would like to thank the volunteer docents of the Covina Valley Historical Society for helping keep the past alive and providing valuable ephemera like Dr. Finch's high school yearbook and written memories of long-time citizens of the City of Covina.

Finally, a shout-out to Stinky, my peach-faced male lovebird, who sat on my left shoulder and reminded me when it was time to clock out at the end of each day.

For More News About Steve Kosareff,
Signup For Our Newsletter:
http://wbp.bz/newsletter

Word-of-mouth is critical to an author's long-
term success. If you appreciated this book please
leave a review on the Amazon sales page:
http://wbp.bz/satinpumpsa

Made in the USA
Las Vegas, NV
04 February 2022

42903365R00174